RADICAL ENCOUNTERS
—— WITH ——
GOD

RADICAL ENCOUNTERS
—— WITH ——
GOD

BY
MELISSA RE-ALFRED

All rights reserved
Second Edition, 2022
© Melissa Re-Alfred, 2021

No part of this publication may be reproduced or stored in a retrieval system, or transmitted in any form by means of electronic, mechanical, photocopying, or otherwise, without prior written permission from the author.

The events and conversations in this book have been set down to the best of the author's ability, although some names and details have been changed to protect the privacy of individuals. Unless otherwise indicated, Scriptures are taken from the Holy Bible, New International Version®, NIV®. Copyright ®

copyright® 1973, 1978, 1984, 2011 by Biblica, Inc.™ Used by permission of Zondervan. All rights reserved worldwide.

www.zondervan.com The "NIV" and "New International

Version" are trademarks in the United States Patent and

Trademark Office by Biblica, Inc.TM
Print Book ISBN: 978-1-7778190-4-0
eBook ISBN: 978-1-7778190-5-7

Dedication

To God, this book would not be possible without you!

To my four beautiful, amazing children, Nation, Jonathan, Caleb, Josiah. You are my greatest gifts, and I am so thankful God allowed me to be your mother!

Contents

Acknowledgments ix
Endorsement Testimonies...x

Introduction 1

Chapter 1
The Name Of JESUS 5

Chapter 2
The Supernatural Realm 15

Chapter 3
Radical Encounters and Testimonies: Part I 33
Supernatural healing at seven...33
A stranger's dream...35
Still small voice 36
What's with the word Nation? 40

Chapter 4
Healing..42

Chapter 5
Radical Encounters and Testimonies Part II.......................60
Run!..60
So, think about it!..64
John 3:16...68

Chapter 6
Dreams and Visions 73

Chapter 7
Radical Encounters and Testimonies Part III 82
Glory balls 82
Angels and wine! 85
Money miracles 87
The ferris wheel angel 89
The vase 91
I'm going to speak to you tonight 93
Your shadow will heal them 95

Chapter 8
The Prophetic 99

Chapter 9
Radical Encounters and Testimonies Part IV 116
They're gone! 116
Bag of shrooms 118
Déjà vu meets word of knowledge on steroids 120
Jonathan's home! 123

Chapter 10
Eyes Up 128

Acknowledgments

To my parents, thank you for all your love and support. Dad, till we meet again in eternity, enjoy Jesus and the coffee up there, I'm sure it's heavenly!

To my beautiful four precious gifts from God, Nation, Jonathan, Caleb, Josiah who came after this book was finished as one of my greatest surprises, I am humbled and honored that God chose me to be your mom. You have been the greatest joys and blessings in life, and I love you so very much and always will. To my husband Sandy, thank you for always speaking life and sharing your gift of faith with me.

To God, Jesus, and Holy Spirit, this book wouldn't even be possible without you! Thank you for your love, friendship, and the gift of unity and salvation, and from the bottom of my heart, thank you for entrusting me with these Radical Encounters. I give you all the glory now and forever!

Endorsement Testimonies

Interpretation of any information is biased by the receiver based upon past experiences, wants, and desires. Even when God speaks or shows us visions, we often need to go to an expert for unbiased interpretation. I can say, personally speaking, Melissa has on several occasions provided not only unbiased interpretation of dreams but often provides details to the dream that were not mentioned. Her accuracy in interpretation and input comes not from the natural knowledge of who I am, as she and I have never met in person, but from a supernatural gift from God.

Karen McAdams Stowe, Mary & Martha Independent Consultant

Melissa has been called for such a time as this to reveal and share radical encounters with God. This book will increase our faith and unlock aspects of our Savior we are rarely given the privilege to experience. She is brave and unorthodox, and the journey she has been on with God and has been chosen to share will allow others to experience a relationship and life meant for radical encounters.

Ruth Lewis, Pastor

The first night I met Melissa, she gave me a specific date that carried significant meaning to me. The second time Melissa gave me a word, she told me that she could see me on stage teaching. Little did Melissa know that word was about ready to manifest in my life. The next week the Lord gave me an opportunity to start a mission for an after-abortion support group/ miscarriage and stillborn support. The date Melissa called out as well ties in significantly, being the exact day, I had a forced abortion as a young teenager. Melissa carries a strong prophetic gift and truly uses the principles of God in her life.

Nicole Shafer, Teacher

Before Melissa even had the chance to know me very well, she spoke several prophetic words and truth into my life. Since these words have been spoken over me, I have moved in more noble boldness and confidence that others can see. I can say that my life has been enriched since these words have been spoken, and I'm grateful for my relationship with Melissa and her strong prophetic God-given gift. She continues to uplift and pour so much into my life and others' lives with willingness and joy regularly; I am not sure if she really knows just how much it has blessed me. Thank you, Melissa!

Kimberly Delay, Sales

Living on the edge of faith and pushing the envelope for the greater things that the Bible talks about is where you will find Melissa. I have known her for ten-plus years and can attest that just getting around her will push you to believe and increase your own personal faith to the next level. I highly recommend this book because I believe it will have a radical impact on your life as you read it. Melissa doesn't come from a place of just head knowledge, she comes from a place of experience and living it out daily, and I am confident that that will be evidently felt and seen as you read this book.

Reginald Aristide, Pastor

Introduction

Hello, I'm so glad a copy of *Radical Encounters with God* has made it into your hands.

I don't believe that happened by chance. And as you read it, you will realize that my book *Radical Encounters with God* is just as described in the title…radical! But if you have read any part of the Bible, you'll know that it lands in good company. Radical encounters were an absolute norm in the life of Jesus and His followers. As you turn the pages, I believe God wants to use this book to draw you closer and increase your faith to believe in radical things. He wants you to no longer have a life of spiritual yo-yoing, one minute up and the next down. He wants you to walk in a life of victory. Despite what›s going on around you, like Jesus in the boat, you're going to be so much at peace and rest that you take a nap even if the wind and the waves are having a tantrum all around.

Recently God spoke to me about this story in the boat in the Bible. He said to me," Melissa, do you realize that Jesus was sleeping because, yes, He wasn't worried, and, yes, because He was at rest and at peace? But, more importantly, He was sleeping because, in the end, He didn't even need the boat in the first place!"

If only the disciples had realized that they didn't need the boat either because they could walk on water just like Jesus, there's a good chance they would have been napping too!

I believe that we're going to see a lot more well-rested Christians and water-walkers rising in this next phase of His kingdom come, His will being done on earth as it is in Heaven, simply because those that know our God shall be strong and do exploits (Daniel 11:32 KJV). You see, "Knowing about God" and "Knowing God" are not the same things. This book is solely about the "Knowing God aspect!"

Throughout the book, I share 33 years of personal encounters, testimonies, and stories starting at a very young age. With each encounter I share, so will another layer of God, His love, and His character be revealed to you.

I have also woven in teachings that will help lay down a biblical foundation for understanding these radical and supernatural encounters. I do that because when testimonies and teaching are coupled together, they can ignite an atomic bomb in the spirit realm and make way for many victories for the kingdom of God.

A heart with understanding is crucial to God, for does He not say in Proverbs 4:7, "*Wisdom is the principal thing, therefore get wisdom: and with all thy getting, get understanding*" (KJV).

As you read this book, you will come to understand who you are and whose you are. The boundaries placed on the impossible will be shattered and replaced with a new understanding of the limitless God.

For those of you who don't yet know God but picked up this book out of curiosity, I believe this will help you experience the true and living God in a very real and personal way. He will speak and make Himself known to you throughout the pages.

For those who already know God and are brothers and sisters in the faith, I believe this book will cause you to leap to the next level. When God levels up, He likes to multiply a thing – not just add to it, so get ready!

And with that, readers, if you are ready to get your world rocked with some radical encounters and teachings, then go ahead and turn this page. See you on the flip side!

Chapter 1

The Name Of JESUS

September 5, 2000 is a day I will never forget.

First, it was exactly three years to that day that I suddenly lost a very close family member, and secondly, it was the day of an out-of-this-world encounter that I'm about to share with you.

But first, a courtesy warning.

This testimony is not exactly all "rainbows and butterflies" but something extremely intense. My mind gets blown away every time I think about it or share it: and it happened to me.

So please consider yourself advised. Shall we? Most nights back then, you would find me hanging out with my friends and having fun. But that day on September 5, 2000, being the third anniversary of the passing of a loved one, I decided to just keep it low-key and stay in. I wasn't really in the mood to go out either. As the day loomed closer, I had already spent a couple of days crying and reminiscing over someone so greatly missed, so much so that by the time the actual anniversary came, I was so spent and there were no more tears left. I just wanted to spend the day in my pajamas, watching movies and not having to think much at all.

So that's what I did all day – lounged in front of the TV. I remember it was around 11:30 pm when I started getting tired. I had made it through the day and was ready to turn off the TV and go to sleep. I settled into bed under my blanket. Just moments away from nodding off and falling asleep, I heard these words, "A demon is about to come into your room." "What?" I thought back, disturbed.

To be honest, I wasn't really asking for any response. When I heard the announcement, oddly enough, it was clear and precise enough for me to believe it. It was the craziest statement, yet somehow, I just knew there was something concrete about it. It wasn't said in panic or an elevated tone, but more in a matter-of-fact kind of way: a demon was about to walk into my room, and I was strangely certain of that!

Now's a good time to pause and say this: over the years, I had experienced certain things in the supernatural, prophetically speaking. For example, I would know when women were pregnant and the gender of their baby; I would have dreams about certain things that would come true; I would meet someone new sometimes and know their exact birthday or get a range and say, "Is your birthday somewhere between April 14 and 18?" …and more. But never in a million years did I imagine I would ever have a face-to-face encounter with a demonic entity. At best, sometimes, I would sense evil in or around a person, and, even then, I wasn't walking around investigating or looking for it. Believe me on that one. I didn't even like horror films and still don't!

But, as it happened, here I was, alone in my room, now wide awake and about to encounter a demon, of all things!

I suddenly, instinctively, knew to look in the direction of the doorway. Sure enough, I saw that demon walk right into the room! I cannot really put into words my shock at seeing this unbelievably evil creature! He was dark and very tall in appearance, I would guess somewhere between seven and eight feet, and scary as all heck. His skin was covered in what looked to be like layers of soot buildup, and his hair and nails –long, dirty, and unkempt –were also covered in layers of soot. He had on a breastplate of sorts that was some kind of silver metal plating covered with short sharp spikes. It looked like he was wearing a pleated skirt of the same material as the breastplate. There was no colour to him, just variations of dark and grays.

As the demon approached, I began having the strangest sensation. The best way I can describe it is being "put under," like when you are given a general anesthetic before surgery. With each step he took towards me, I was becoming more and more drowsy as if I was counting downwards from 100, 99, 98, 97, 96, 9…and then…BOOM…I was out. My eyes closed just as he neared my bedside, and then I faded out. I had no control over it whatsoever.

The next thing I remember is standing in a very dark place. Not dark as in after midnight, and no lights are on. No, this was darkness with zero traces of light," pure" darkness without cracks, rips, or tears to it. It was the darkest place, space, location, atmosphere I had ever been in or ever knew existed.

Suddenly, while in this space, I could hear faint sounds in the far distance. Just a jumble of noises at first, hard to make out, but after a few minutes, all was silent again. Then after a short pause, like someone had pressed rewind on a VHS tape (yes, I'm VHS tape old), the distant noise was now closer, and it was clear to me what I was hearing. It was the sound of a car driving at high speed for what seemed like a minute or so, and then this horrible sound of metal smashing as if the car had crashed. The sound and the imagined scene brought a sense of fear and panic. Although I could see nothing, there was something so real about it that all my senses were heightened.

Then all went quiet again. Moments later, the sound started all over again, but this time it was much closer to me, now all on top of me. It was torturous, like living in a constant loop with increased intensity each time and no exit to escape. Thankfully, after the third time of this play-rewind- replay, I was abruptly whisked away to an entirely different scene.

I now found myself standing in the middle of a beautiful meadow, surrounded by tall grass, with a nearby river and blue skies above. Again, I can't explain how this happened or why...but here I was, transported from this very dark place to a light one. As I took it all in, I noticed the tall grass swaying a little by the gentle breeze, and a few men spread out in the grass, all standing there looking at me with peaceful countenance. I didn't recognize them from before, but they had an "ancient" look about them. I had a feeling that they were from another place and might have been angels or some sort of heavenly beings. They were all wearing the same outfit, long beige robes.

I stayed in this blissful place for a few moments drinking it all in, before—without warning—I was back in my room. Now I was fully awake and no longer in a state of unconsciousness, but very alert. To my horror, the demon was still in the room. Not only still in the room, but now standing right beside me and about to do the most unreal thing imaginable.

The demon reached out with both hands and started to press his way into my side, slowly at first with his long creepy fingernails followed by the palms of his hands. I wasn't in pain; it felt more like extreme discomfort. His hands continued to move into my side until they stopped right around the middle of my stomach area and clenched down as I felt them grip me.

Now, this part gets really trippy, so stay with me. It wasn't the physical me that he had grabbed hold of; it was my soul. How did I know that? I am not certain, but it would seem that our souls can be found in the center of our bodies. It makes me think about what Jesus said in John 7:38, *"He that believeth on me, as the scripture hath said, out of his belly shall flow rivers of living water"* (KJV). There is a connection between the "here" and the "there" that can be found in the middle of our beings. Sometimes as the Spirit moves over you, you can feel a "pulling" sensation in the center of your being. Some of you, even as you are reading this, know what I'm talking about. It's also the place in the natural where all life begins and is conceived, so it makes sense that there would be similarities in the supernatural as well.

As the demon had a firm hold on my soul, he started to pull me out of my body. I felt "me" coming out of me. It was the most unsettling feeling. My body was still lying on the bed, not moving, but at the same time, I, Melissa, was moving out of my body, and I had no power within myself to stop what was happening. My mind was spinning. How in the world could this even be real? And yet, here I was moving off my bed, as a very large spine-chilling creature was pulling out my soul.

And, please, let me just pause right here for a second time before I continue because I know what some of you might be thinking. This sounds completely mad, something you might see out of a Stephen King film. You're right; it absolutely does. I would think the same thing myself had it not happened to me.

But here's the thing: something very supernatural was taking place, defying the natural laws of physics, time, and space. The Oxford dictionary describes "supernatural" as *a manifestation or event attributed to some force beyond scientific understanding or the laws of nature*. It's totally beyond what we can make sense of in the natural.

As I was being pulled out of my body, which seemed to be in slow motion, I began scrambling for help! I mean, what is one to do in a case like this? If there was even a chance, would I call 911? Phone a friend. Maybe find a "lifeline" somewhere? Scream for my mom and my stepdad, who were in the next room? Did I tell them a demon from hell was pulling me out of my body when they came running in? I mean, what were my options here? How could I fix this? Then, suddenly, the thought came to me – in the most casual way, given the circumstances: "Call for Jesus!" Immediately I felt, "YES, THAT'S IT!"

I wasn't going to church at the time, but I had known of Jesus since childhood and would think about Him and feel His presence, too, from time to time throughout my teenage years and now into young adulthood. I would recite the "Now I lay me down to sleep" prayer whenever I felt scared; that's that. HA! In those days, that was pretty much the extent of my relationship with God.

So, without any time to spare, I quickly ventured to call upon Jesus for help.

Much to my surprise and dismay, nothing came out of my mouth! Now I became aware that my breath was leaving me, and I was incapable of saying anything. No one tells you that if ever you find yourself being pulled out of your body by a demon, you can expect to lose your breath as well.

In that moment, if horror and terror had a baby, that would be the level of panic, fear, and dread you would have found in me. I didn't know why this was happening to me or what the demon planned to do once he finished pulling me out of my body. Would I ever return? I was completely and utterly helpless. I thought my parents were going to wake up in the morning and find me, well," gone."

With only moments left before I was all the way pulled out of my body, one last thought came to mind, a "Hail Mary" moment, my last-ditch attempt before the inevitable. I was going to call on Jesus with my thoughts, for that was all I seemed to have left – the only thing I still had control over. If this didn't work, all was lost!

So, with all that I had left in me, I SCREAMED THE NAME OF JESUS in my mind and cried with every ounce of my being: "J.E.S.U.S!"

Before I even finished pushing out the last "S" in His name, I was 100% back in my body, and the demon was gone! Vanished! I imagine He must have defecated out of terror at the very glimpse of Jesus. I think about the legion of demons that Jesus confronted in Mark 5:1-20, who fell on their knees and begged Jesus not to torture them. Jesus has more power in one strand of hair than all of hell put together, infinite times over.

So here I was again, still lying on my bed in complete shock, my thoughts just swirling. My soul was back in my body. The demon that came to get me was gone because Jesus had come down from heaven to save me. My earthly mind could not find an explanation quick enough to help calm me down, but, as God would have it, my night of surprises had more to come!

I felt something touch my lips, causing them to tingle and vibrate fiercely. This powerful vibrating sensation on my lips spread quickly to the top of my head and down to the bottom of my feet – like a bullet being shot out of a barrel. It felt as if one big jolt of electricity was buzzing through my body, seeming to intensify more and more, not just a little, but the electrical charge would jump up in intensity by levels. It wasn't painful but was super intense, and I wasn't sure how I could contain it all, but I know that it was the pure raw power of God Himself shooting through my veins and entire body. Then, just as it came, it was all gone. All of it!

The room just simply went back to normal. There was nothing left of the heaven and hell showdown. Suddenly all was still. I was glued to my bed, unable to move at this point! I wanted so badly to get up and run like Forrest Gump right out of there, but I just couldn't summon up the strength to lift myself.

When I was finally able to move, I ran downstairs, called my dad on the phone, and told him what had happened. I don't remember what he said, but I'm sure he was trying to reassure me that I was safe, and everything would be okay.

Before reading this book, not many people would have known about this radical encounter. Only a handful of people close to me knew. Many years later, I was asked by one of the pastors at the church we were attending in Ottawa to share it before a few hundred people who were at this particular weekly meeting. People I had known for over ten years came up to me in shock because they were hearing about this radical encounter for the first time. I just didn't walk around announcing this event as I went about my day. Nevertheless, I give God all the glory as I share it with you and others now.

Here's the thing: I didn't sign up for this, nor would I have volunteered had I been asked – no one could pay me enough! But, looking back, I am thankful that I got to see and learn firsthand about the powerful name of **JESUS!** Thank God, as I learned in my case, it's so powerful that just thinking it with all my being was enough to destroy the works of darkness and save me! There's nowhere God cannot deliver you from; there's no corner of the earth, no place too high or low He can't reach to get you. Even if you make your bed in hell, He can find you there (Psalm 139:8).

So, I leave this chapter with the question, "Is there anything too hard for the Lord?" I'm going to have to give it a hard, "No!" Nothing is too hard or impossible for the Lord!

How does one explain a supernatural encounter or use science to explain it? You can't! Throughout Bible history, people have experienced the supernatural, and people are still doing so to this day. We can, in fact, expect to see more supernatural signs and wonders in these last days. Acts 2:13

The whole of chapter 2 is dedicated to all-things-supernatural, where I explore the subject more deeply. I think it's essential to lay down a biblical foundation and gain some understanding as a follow-up to an encounter such as this one. There are many other encounters, testimonies, and stories that I share in this book, but for now, let's investigate the dimension of the supernatural.

Chapter 2

The Supernatural Realm

As I mentioned in the previous chapter, I want to add some valuable biblical teaching to these supernatural and radical encounters, testimonies, and stories. Throughout the book, I have woven in teaching chapters to help lay down a biblical foundation for these radical testimonies, encounters and stories that I'm sharing with you. We are going to be diving into the subject of dreams, visions, prophecy, hearing God's voice, discernment, deliverance, angels, demons, healing, signs, wonders, miracles, and the supernatural, as I lay a biblical foundation for such phenomena.

A lot of these things are intertwined with each other and help us to understand what is taking place. You will see this as I share other supernatural testimonies and experiences with you in later chapters of the book. As you become more familiar with such things, you will even start to recognize whether they came from God or not.

We will start with the supernatural because, to me, all the others fall under the umbrella of the supernatural. Without the supernatural, there would be no signs, wonders, miracles, healings, prophecy, and other amazing things. I will also teach about angels, demons, and of course, heaven, for all these are all part of the supernatural realm.

Here's the exciting news: if you like my book so far, then I believe you will love the teaching chapters as well. I will be using the Bible to anchor biblical truths that underpin the supernatural in an easy-to-understand way.

And, if you find that my teaching/writing style is casual, you won't be wrong – it's just the way I am and how God made me. If my teaching style was an outfit, it would be jeans and a hoodie, making it comfortable for a lot of people to relate to.

One of the many, many cool things about the Bible is that the whole book is full of supernatural stories and encounters literally from cover to cover, starting with Genesis Chapter 1:1, "In the Beginning God spoke…" and it was. Right out the gate, we are totally introduced to the supernatural GOD who said, "Let there be light, and there was light!" That's quite the benchmark to start with, right?

In the Bible, there are so many biblical experiences to pull from, and I highly doubt if we will touch even 0.000000000000000001% of them in my book. Jesus didn't even cover in His teaching even 1% of all the supernatural, signs, wonders, healings, and miracles in the Bible during His ministry on earth. John, one of Jesus' closest disciples tells us in John 21:25, *"Jesus did many other things as well. If every one of them were written down, I suppose that even the whole world would not have room for the books that would be written."* To me, our beautiful planet seems so big, and yet it isn't big enough to house all the books that it would take to write and recount all the amazing things Jesus did along with His encounters during His short thirty-three years on planet earth and three years in active ministry.

When Jesus first came to earth through His miraculous birth, He gave up His wealth and majesty so we could gain it all. Sometimes when people hear the scripture that Jesus became poor so that we might become rich (2 Corinthians 8:9), they think it means He was financially broke when He was here on earth. They then go on to teach that Christians should live a life of being broke as well and give all they have to others and live with holes in their shoes and rips in their jeans, and not in the cool way either, as if that somehow makes us like Jesus. I'm pretty sure Jesus and His family were quite well off in His day from His carpenter's trade. Jesus after all was known as the son of the carpenter, Joseph, who everyone knew as the go-to man for all things carpentry. They were well known in the city because of their family business.

I'm all for giving to those in need, as we should, but that's not what 2 Corinthians 8:9 means. It's referring to the fact that the minute Jesus stepped out of Heaven to come to earth and make it His temporary home for the next 33 years, He became instantly poor. Anything outside of heaven is considered poor!

With all his worldly wealth, Bill Gates is considered poor compared to a blade of grass in heaven. Sounds wild, doesn't it? But seriously, I've seen a blade of grass in heaven during a dream visitation there once. I was totally mesmerized by the grass there. Of all the things in the landscape of heaven, it was the grass that got me so transfixed; I could have stayed there for days just admiring it. The greenish-blue colors were out of this world, like no color I'd ever seen before! And it had a way about it: it was ALIVE with no sense of fading or trace of death in it whatsoever.

Can you fathom it? If that's just the grass in heaven, how much more amazing is the rest? I mean, for example, one of our most valuable commodities on earth is gold. In heaven, you'll find lots of gold there too. Heaven is so full of it; you'll even find it as pavement! They aren't called "Streets of gold" for nothing. (Revelation 21:21)

Heaven is just so above and beyond anything we could possibly imagine. You can go from one place to another in a split second. There can be more than one thing taking up a single "space" as things and objects can be layered. Jesus' walking through a wall after His glorious resurrection is an example of that. You can communicate with people and angels in heaven through your thoughts! Yep, mind-reading – heaven did it first! You don't age or get sick because there is no death or dying there, not even stubbing your toe by accident. You can even fly in heaven if you want. Heaven is one big giant supernatural playground with so many things to discover, it will take you all of eternity to do so.

But let's rewind just a bit more. The supernatural, what exactly is that?

The supernatural, simply put, is a realm like the one we are in now, minus the laws of time and space. This is not to say you can't experience time or space there – it's the supernatural after all! I wouldn't rule it out. But it's not governed by the framework we have here, with the sun rising and falling day by day, with years passing by, and the aging process in motion.

Much like the natural realm, the supernatural realm is made by God and for God. Psalm 118:24 says, *"This is the day that the Lord has made..."* (ESV), and Colossians 1:16 says, *"...for through him God created everything in the heavenly realms and on earth. He made the things we can see and the things we can't see – such as thrones, kingdoms, rulers, and authorities in the unseen world. Everything was created through him and for him"* (NLT).

I mean, there are just layers and layers to this thing and the unseen realm. God is awesome in His creations. At times He draws us into the supernatural realm in different ways to share, talk, impart, guide, lead, comfort, heal, or just simply love on us. At times it will be angels that you encounter sent by God. Not because He's too busy to do it Himself or you are at the bottom of His "favorites" list, so He hands us off to the angels. Listen, God can have five billion conversations with five billion different people all at the same time. He's just being GOD like that! In no way is He too busy for you. But I think He does send angels sometimes because He wants us to know we not only have Him as a loving heavenly father, but we also have amazing supernatural friends and created beings such as angels pulling for us. Friend, you are never alone!

Angel facts: they are too vast in number to count and can take on many different forms. You and I may have even entertained angels unawares because the Bible tells us they visited Abram in his tent in the appearance of men (Hebrews 13:2). They could look just like us, and we wouldn't even know it was an angel unless Holy Spirit revealed it to us.

There are different kinds of angels created with different purposes and different ranks (2 Corinthians 10:4-5). They also have names and personalities just like you and me. Some of the more "common" angel groups known to us are Seraphim, Cherubim, and Archangels. Seraphim are mentioned in Isaiah's vision:

In the year that King Uzziah died, I saw [in a vision] the Lord sitting on a throne, high and exalted, with the train of His royal robe filling the [most holy part of the] temple. Above Him seraphim (heavenly beings) stood; each one had six wings: with two wings he covered his face, with two wings he covered his feet, and with two wings he flew. And one called out to another, saying, "Holy, Holy, Holy is the LORD of hosts.

The whole earth is filled with His glory." And the foundations of the thresholds trembled at the voice of him who called out, and the temple was filling with smoke. Then I said, "Woe is me! For I am ruined, Because I am a man of [ceremonially] unclean lips, And I live among a people of unclean lips; For my eyes have seen the King, the LORD of hosts."

Then one of the seraphim flew to me with a burning coal in his hand, which he had taken from the altar with tongs. He touched my mouth with it and said, "Listen carefully, this has touched your lips; your wickedness [your sin, your injustice, your wrongdoing] is taken away and your sin atoned for and forgiven" (Isaiah 6:1-7 AMP).

When I read this last part of the vision, I could not help but connect with how Isaiah's lips were touched and how mine were also touched during the radical encounter I had, as described in the previous chapter. I would think to myself, "Man, how strange that my lips would be the first thing to be touched in such an incredibly intense moment like that!" You may have thought the same as you were reading it. Humanly speaking, this seemed odd to me; we just don't go around touching people's lips. And, frankly, if ever I had to guess what part of my body God would touch first, I would have gone with something more along the lines of the top of my head or my shoulders – but lips came as a big surprise to me.

But then, to find out here that Isaiah had a similar experience during his supernatural encounter via a vision was such a revelation. It emphasized the need to cleanse our speech before all else. Jeremiah, a prophet as well, had his lips touched by God Himself also (Jeremiah 1:9).

Cherubim angels have a special place too. You will find one standing at the entrance of the Garden of Eden, still to this day, I'm sure. In Genesis 3:24, we see that cherubim with a flaming sword were assigned to guard the Garden of Eden: *So GOD drove the man out (Adam and Eve) and at the east of the Garden of Eden He (permanently) stationed the cherubim and the sword with the flashing blade which turned round and round (in every direction) to protect and guard the way (entrance, access) to the tree of life* (AMP).

You can find a detailed *description* of these cherubim in Ezekiel 1, verse 10. That includes multiple faces, hands like a human, and six wings. What a sight, eh!

God also picked cherub to be the two angels represented over the Ark of the Covenant, one on either side with their wings stretched out in a covering or protecting kind of way. Cherubim seem to be used often to guard and protect.

Archangels are high-level angels. "Archangel" means "chief of the angels." We know that Michael is the chief of the host of heaven, the army, and military angels. Revelation 12:7-9 says, *"Then war broke out in heaven. Michael and his angels fought against the dragon, and the dragon and his angels fought back. But he was not strong enough, and they lost their place in heaven. The great dragon was hurled down—that ancient serpent called the devil, or Satan, who leads the whole world astray. He was hurled to the earth, and his angels with him."*

Gabriel, another archangel mentioned in the Bible, is the head of the messenger angels. In Luke chapter 1, Gabriel came to Mary to tell the amazing news that she had found favor with the Lord and would birth the world's Savior, Jesus!

What an honor that must have been! The good news is that, because of what Jesus did on the cross, now we all can carry Jesus in us, through the Holy Spirit. Obviously, unlike Mary, who carried Him in the natural world, we carry Him in the supernatural through our spirit, which supersedes the natural realm. This is why you can witness and or experience manifestations of your own like miracles, healing, signs and wonders and more, in your physical body and the natural realm.

Even peace can be a supernatural manifestation of God. I once had a 3.5-month encounter with peace – not regular peace – but the peace that "surpasses all understanding" kind of peace mentioned in the Bible. Let me digress for a minute here. When I heard the gospel preached by John Crowder at a weekend conference in 2011, it was preached in such a powerful and new way that I believe the gospel was meant to be shared as a free gift from God. The gospel and salvation are not something that we can earn by good works or even add to. They are already perfect just the way they are. Jesus did such an amazing job of being our Savior all by Himself. *"For it is by grace you have been saved, through faith--and this is not from yourselves, it is the gift of God"* (Ephesians 2:8). No amount of our fasting or praying, reading the Bible, or good deeds –although these things are beneficial- can add to what Jesus solely accomplished on the cross.

I mean, what would happen if we missed a day of praying, fasting, or reading our Bible? What if we said a bad word or got angry at our spouse? Would we lose our salvation? What if we got back on track the next day and did everything right and checked off all the Christian boxes? Would we be saved again? If so, for how long? One week, maybe two? If we did it well, maybe a whole month? Then would we have to do it all over again to make sure we are saved for the next few weeks, and so on and so on?

You didn't clean yourself off and make yourself righteous by your own efforts and works. *"For just as through the disobedience of the one man the many were made sinners, so also through the obedience of the one man the many will be made righteous"* (Romans 5:19). It's based on something Jesus has already done, and the credit and glory will always be reserved for Him and Him alone.

I have spent hours and hours in the word of God and praying at times, gone on month-long fasts, and more. But it's important to know why you are doing these things; if it's to gain something Jesus already gave you for free, you may want to revisit your why. *"For what the law was powerless to do because it was weakened by the flesh, God did by sending his own Son in the likeness of sinful flesh to a sin offering, and so he condemned sin in the flesh"* (Romans 8:3).

Once you get a clear understanding of the cross and Him crucified in your soul and what that means for you, then there really is another kind of peace out there, a genuine and supernatural kind that will have you walking through life anchored in His rest. A place of peace because of understanding that allows such a friendship with God never experienced and without the hindrance of guilt, shame, or being downcast. It's like peace on steroids, and it's so good! I want to live in a lifelong peace encounter. If I strive at anything in life, I strive in this: to live out all the benefits that the death and resurrection of Jesus Christ our Lord and Savior paid for. Great peace is one of those benefits.

Coming back to Angels: although there are different kinds of angels with different job functions or tasks, they all have the same agenda in the end. Hebrews 1:14 tells us they all are ministering spirits sent out to serve those who are to inherit salvation. Honestly, how blessed we are!

Check out this passage of scripture in 2 Kings 6:15-17 from the Life Application Bible. When Elisha, the prophet's servant, got up early one morning and went outside, there were enemy troops, horses, and chariots everywhere. *"Alas, my master, what shall we do now?"* he cried out to Elisha.

"Don't be afraid!" Elisha told him. *"For our army is bigger than theirs!"* Then Elisha prayed, *"Lord, open his eyes and let him see!"*

And the Lord opened the young man's eyes so he could see horses and chariots of fire everywhere upon the mountain! We have some mighty friends out there, guys!

In the supernatural, you may also encounter demons — even a few thousand— also known as Legion. Mark 5:8. Do not worry, though, for if you are a believer, no weapon formed against you shall prosper! (Isaiah 54:17). The keywords here are "Don't worry!" Fear will mess you up. Try not to fall into its trap. I once heard someone say the phrase "fear not" is found in the bible three hundred and sixty-five times. One "fear not" for every day of the year. GOD doesn't want us to spend our days in fear.

You see, Jesus knows it, demons know it, and by gosh golly it would serve us so much better if we knew it too!

The reason why you might see demons is that before they were demons, they were angels living in the supernatural realm as created beings that live for eternity. *"…and they can no longer die; for they are like the angels. They are God's children, since they are children of the resurrection"* (Luke 20:36). Even you and I will live forever and ever once we finally leave this natural realm.

Now the enemy is trying his hardest to bring as many people down with him as he can during whatever little time he has left! He once tasted the sweetness of God and His closeness. That's now something you and I get to enjoy. He hates that he lost that place and will spend his time trying to make sure others don't get to it either. The adage" misery loves company" may have started with Satan. Satan hates God and would do anything to try and stick it where it hurts. He knows you are God's beloved, and it would hurt God not to have you in Heaven with Him for all of eternity.

But, while we are on this earth in time, we might catch a glimpse of him in the supernatural or even in a full-on encounter in the real world. He comes to kill, steal, and destroy.

It doesn't mean he'll succeed in those things; it just means we know what his "day job" is. When trying to do so, he uses lies and deception as his go-to. He is not called "the father of lies" for no reason. Your best defense is to know the word of GOD and hold your ground. If you do, he will wear himself out and flee. James 4:7 says, *"Submit yourselves, then, to God. Resist the devil, and he will flee from you."* With every lie Satan spew's, there is a truth to counter it.

Recently I woke up from a dream, and I heard the LORD say, "The enemy doesn't have the resources to take you out. I stripped him of all power, and the only thing left is lies!" Not long after that, I was pondering the scripture in 1 Peter 5:8: *"Be sober, be vigilant; because your adversary the devil walks about like a roaring lion, seeking whom he may devour"* (NKJV). As I was doing so, God spoke to me and said, "Let him know he MAY NOT devour you!"

I was like, "Yes, God! You don't have to tell me twice." We are heirs and joint heirs with Christ Jesus, and He has given us dominion on this earth. The devil walks around seeking who has permitted him to devour. Let him know right now he doesn't have your permission, and he MAY NOT devour you either! Being sober minded also means mentally remembering who you are. Clearly and soberly remember the fact that you are a child of the Most High God, every day and in every situation.

You are God's very dream come true. He thought of you, every single detail of you, long before you took your first breath. Way before you came to life in your mother's womb, at that very first second of conception, you were already God's creation (Jeremiah 1:5). You are His very much prized handiwork (Ephesians 2:10).

Know that demons were once angels who ended up going rogue and were cast out of Heaven. While still God's angels, they were faced with a choice offered by Satan, whose name was Lucifer, to decide their eternal fate. Lucifer, a beautiful cherub, was so awed by his own beauty and talents that he desired to be as God and take his place above the Highest.

> *How you have fallen from heaven,*
> *morning star, son of the dawn!*
> *You have been cast down to the earth,*
> *you who once laid low the nations!*
> *You said in your heart,*
> *"I will ascend to the heavens;*
> *I will raise my throne*
> *above the stars of God;*
> *I will sit enthroned on the mount of assembly,*
> *on the utmost heights of Mount Zaphon*
> *I will ascend above the tops of the clouds;*
> *I will make myself like the Most High."*
> *But you are brought down to the realm of the dead,*
> *to the depths of the pit*

(Isaiah 14:12-15).

When Satan fell (Revelation 12:4), a third of the angels chose to go with him. That means two-thirds were left in Heaven and remained faithful and loyal to God. This also means that for every demon, there are at least two angels. I know what some of you are thinking, "Only two angels for every one demon? Is that going to be enough?" I know because the enemy tried to spoon-feed me that lie once too. That is also in part, sadly, because some preachers are heavy on Satan in their teaching and light on Jesus. Have you ever been to a church where Sunday after Sunday, all that is shared from the pulpit is focused on the enemy and his tactics to take you out? If so, then, of course, you are going to be thinking like this; you've been conditioned too. But Hebrews 12:22 talks of an *"innumerable company of angels"* (KJV), and Daniel, describing God on the throne, says: *"Thousands upon thousands attended him; ten thousand times ten thousand stood before him"* (Daniel 7:10).

At any rate, this level of thinking is dangerous because it puts more faith in the devil's agenda to harm than the finished work of the Cross to save. Do we believe more in Adam's ability to bring sin into the world than in Jesus' ability to free us from it? *"And having disarmed the powers and authorities, he made a public spectacle of them, triumphing over them by the cross"* (Colossians 2:15). I also like the way the Mirror Word Bible puts it: *"His brilliant victory made a public spectacle of them. That means every ruler and authority empowered by the devil after the fall of Adam. The voice of the cross will never be silenced!"* Okay, one more translation, because it's just that good! *"He stripped all the spiritual tyrants in the universe of their sham authority at the Cross and marched them naked through the street"* (The Message Bible).

In other words, Jesus humiliated the devil in the worst way and publicly too, in front of every one of his minions and those watching in Heaven and below. You see, the enemy loves the attention; he loves an audience. Well, that day, I would say he got both attention and audience, just not in the way he would have wanted.

So, back to my point, if just you or I alone can chase one thousand demons and two can chase ten thousand

(Deuteronomy 32:30), then, trust me, one angel, let alone thousands upon thousands, is more than enough!

If you ever find yourself in a situation where you encounter the demonic, remember you are encountering an already defeated foe. Things change dramatically when you know and understand that. Although we don't focus all our attention on the enemy, we need to place our attention where it better belongs on Jesus! I will share with you what God told me to do early this year while I was still in the process of writing this book. He asked me to add the word "defeated" into the sentence in conversations where Satan was mentioned. So, it looks and or sounds like this, defeated enemy or defeated Satan.

I believe there is a wake-up call happening in the body of Christ to the fact that the enemy is under our feet in a real way. As we add the word "defeated" in the conversation, we bring the reality of his defeated-ness back to mind every single time. Too often, Christians are talking about how the devil is attacking them or is after them, and you can hear the fear in their voice. Sadly, they put weight on Satan's ability to attack rather than God's ability to defeat him and his plans. Due to wrong teaching and focus, you can find a lot of that happening to those who are especially steeped in religion and not in relationship with God. Many conversations will become Satan-focused and Jesus-forgotten. That's what happens when you have a form of godliness but deny the power thereof (2 Timothy 3:5). It's this lukewarm-ness that God hates and wants to vomit out of His mouth. (Revelation 3:16)

Here's the deal: the next time you speak about such things, I invite you to say it like this instead, "The DEFEATED devil is after me" or "The DEFEATED enemy is attacking me." See how that makes a world of difference when you put it in the right perspective? It's how I now address the enemy myself.

The Bible has some very radical supernatural stories and experiences to draw inspiration from. The following are some amazing incidents that I personally love.

Moses parting the Red Sea with a rod, how crazy (Exodus 14:21)! Not your average rod, eh? Or the time when Joshua was in battle with the Amorites, and he prayed to the Lord to have the sun and moon stand still so they could finish off the enemy – and both the sun and the moon remained still for a whole day, unmoved (Joshua 10:1-15)! Wow! I mean, for Joshua to even know he could go to God and ask for a thing like that says a lot to me about their relationship. To go to God, first you must believe He is, but still, that's a high-level request right there.

Remember the time when Jesus joined Shadrach, Meshach, and Abednego in the fiery furnace, no doubt having a dance party (Daniel 3:16-21)?

Another amazing story is when Elijah had a standoff to see which God was GOAT, aka "Greatest of All Time." 1 Kings 18, which describes the prophet Elijah's confrontation with the prophets of Baal is such an awesome story. Here's the highlight reel from verses 21-39 MSG:

Elijah challenged the people: "How long are you going to sit on the fence? If God is the real God, follow him; if it's Baal, follow him. Make up your minds!"

Nobody said a word; nobody made a move.

Then Elijah said, "I'm the only prophet of God left in Israel; and there are 450 prophets of Baal. Let the Baal prophets bring up two oxen; let them pick one, butcher it, and lay it out on an altar on firewood-but don't ignite it. I'll take the other ox, cut it up, and lay it on the wood. But neither will I light the fire. Then you pray to your gods, and I'll pray to GOD. The god who answers with fire will prove to be, in fact, God." All the people agreed: "A good plan-do it!"

Elijah told the Baal prophets, "Choose your ox and prepare it. You go first, you're the majority. Then pray to your god, but don't light the fire."

So, they took the ox he had given them, prepared it for the altar, then prayed to Baal. They prayed all morning long, "O Baal, answer us! But nothing happened-not so much as a whisper of breeze. Desperate, they jumped and stomped on the altar they had made.

By noon, Elijah had started making fun of them, taunting, "Call a little louder-he is a god, after all. Maybe he's off meditating somewhere or other, or maybe he's gotten involved in a project or maybe he's on vacation. You don't suppose he's overslept, do you, and needs to be woken up?" They prayed louder and louder, cutting themselves with swords and knives-a ritual common to them-until they were covered in blood.

This went on until well past noon. They used every religious trick and strategy they knew to make something happen on the altar, but nothing happened -not so much as a whisper, not a flicker of response.

Then Elijah told the people, "Enough of that-it's my turn. Gather around." And they gathered. He then put the altar back together for by now it was in ruins. Elijah took twelve stones, one for each of the tribes of Jacob, the same Jacob to whom

GOD has said, "From now on your name is Israel." He built the stones into the altar in honor of GOD. Then Elijah dug a wide trench around the altar. He laid firewood on the altar, cut up the ox, put it on the wood, and said, "Fill four buckets with water and drench both the ox and the firewood." Then he said, "Do it again," and they did it. Then he said, "Do it a third time," and they did it a third time. Their altar was drenched, and the trench was filled with water.

When it was time for the sacrifice to be offered, Elijah the prophet came up and prayed, "O God, God of Abraham, Isaac, and Israel, make it known right now that you are God in Israel, that I am your servant, and that I'm doing what I'm doing under your orders. Answer me, GOD; O answer me and reveal to these people that you are GOD, the true God, and that you are giving these people another chance at repentance.

Immediately the fire of GOD fell and burned up the offering, the wood, the stones, the dirt and even the water in the trench.

All the people saw it happen and fell on their faces in awed worship, exclaiming, "GOD is the true God!" GOD is the true God!" I love that one! How about you?

Most of all, remember your own salvation: how you suddenly turned from darkness to light. Surely that's the very best supernatural encounter you could have ever had!

Chapter 3

Radical Encounters and Testimonies Part 1

SUPERNATURAL HEALING AT SEVEN

When I was young, I had a lot of problems with my earlobe. Now that might sound like something small, but it became a real "thorn in my side," if you will. I had wanted earrings as a little girl, but it didn't go so well. My mom took me to the ear-piercing store to get my ears pierced with some cute studded little girl earrings, which ended up landing me in the hospital. The lady that was doing the piercing was using an ear-piercing gun, and as she held up the gun to my earlobe, she pulled the trigger too hard, and the front earring got lodged in the middle of my earlobe while being held in place by the back part. The next thing I knew, I was at the hospital being wheeled into the surgical room. Obviously, they had to cut it out.

But from then on, my earlobe kept getting infected. It was a cycle of filling up with pus and blood that needed to be drained and squeezed out all the time, and then it filled back up again some short time after. Just when I would think it was healed, it would painfully swell all over again despite creams and medicine. This went on for months. One night my brother and I were at my dad's house (my parents were divorced, and we would go back and forth) and the throbbing pain from my earlobe once again had woken me up in the middle of the night. I crawled out of bed and sat down on the couch in the living room in the middle of the night, crying and feeling tired of it all and feeling a little hopeless. Nothing was working long-term or giving me much relief. At school, I was in pain; at home, I was in pain. I remember as I sat there, that I started to pray to God while holding my earlobe.

My grandmother Rosalie would read bible stories to my brother and me before she passed away, not too long before this. She would read until her jaw got sore from reading, and we loved to hear the stories. I also felt God as a child and knew that He was close to me. Here I was in the middle of the night praying to God, gently holding my earlobe, asking Him to take this pain away and heal me because I knew that He could! It seemed like I was praying for three or four minutes when my prayer was interrupted suddenly. Abruptly I felt my fingers over my earlobe move closer together. I sat there in shock! My earlobe was completely back to normal. The swelling was gone, the pain was gone, and the pus and infection were gone too – all gone, as in disappeared! Dematerialized! There was no trace of the infection anywhere. It was a miracle! And I've never had pain in my earlobe since. Praise God for caring about us so deeply, for having compassion on us all, and for hearing our prayers when we cry out to Him. He is a friend that sticks closer than a brother. He is a good, good Father. (Hebrews 13:5)

A STRANGER'S DREAM

My first job ever was working in a cute little coffee bar in the middle of a flea market. I worked every weekend. Late in the summer of 1997 was a particularly dark time in my life as a teenager. I did a lot of things to try and numb myself from the emotional pain I was in. One Saturday afternoon, my boss introduced me to a friend that had come to the market to visit her. Nothing was unusual about the introduction. It was short, sweet, and polite, and she seemed like a nice lady. I took over the coffee booth while my boss took some time to catch up with her friend. My boss came back shortly after, and we finished the day. I was back at work the next day, but it would prove to be an unusual day.

My boss's friend came by again, but this time it was to see me. She asked to speak with me privately. Once we were in a quiet space, she told me that she hadn't slept much the night before. She had a dream about me where she saw God and me walking together hand in hand; we were very close, and He loved me deeply. After she woke up, God kept pouring into her how much He loved me and how we were going to be close; He wanted her to come back and tell me this.

I was so astonished and touched by it. I wasn't even sure God was interested in me, much less that he thought about me and shared it with a stranger in such a way to keep her up all night. Most of those days surrounding the time of my friend's sudden passing were a blur, but this moment cut right through and left a mark on my heart. That being noticed by God was so needed for me at the time, something that I would come to remember and appreciate often.

God will bug a stranger on your behalf. In the book of Jeremiah, one thing that stands out for me is that God is always trying to reach His people to have a breakthrough with them. Even though they behaved horribly towards Him to the point where it says even the Heavens shrank back in horror and dismay (Jeremiah 2:12 TLB), God was always thinking of ways to try and steer people back to Him. He is relentless in His pursuit of you.

STILL SMALL VOICE

One afternoon when I was in my mid-20s, a few of us were scheduled to go to a meet-up work event. It was one of my first events like that, as I was still new in my career. However, my mentor knew all the who's who in the field and ended up knowing every single person who attended this event.

As it turned out, they were all women, who all happened to be Christians. It didn't take long for conversations to be headed in a God direction, which evolved spontaneously into basically a prayer meeting of all things, right there at this midday work event. It's not every day in a secular place of business that we see that happening, now do we.

I remember we were all sitting at this table holding hands while each one would take turns praying, except for me; I was new to the church scene and still growing in God. Just the thought of praying out loud in front of a bunch of strangers was giving me anxiety, not to mention feeling like a fish out of water in this new career setting too. The last thing I wanted was to feel dumb in front of these well-respected women who had been in this career for quite some time.

During the prayer, however, oddly enough, I kept being drawn to this one lady on the far side of the circle. I tried my best to keep my eyes closed and brush off the urge to look at her, but I couldn't help noticing her, nor could I explain the reason. She looked very well put together, nothing out of the ordinary that would keep drawing my eye, but still, I couldn't seem to help it. Suddenly, as my attention was continuously being drawn in her direction, I heard within my spirit a very tiny, still, small voice that said I was to pray for her. It was so small that I wasn't even sure I heard it right. Nothing changed in the manner or tone it was said, but I did hear it, again and again, a few more times as I zoomed in to pay very close attention within. Along with hearing I was to pray for her, I also now had the prompting that it was for her and her immediate family, specifically in the area of protection.

Even then, though, I was still questioning if I heard it right. As this little impromptu prayer meeting was starting to wrap up, I had a choice to make. I could step out of the boat and approach her, or I could squash it and be on my merry little way. As much as I feared making a fool of myself in case, I was wrong or looked dumb, I was willing to risk it for Him.

To add another layer to this peculiar situation, her sister was also in the biz and was there as well. We had learned that they were both set to leave on a cruise the next day, just the two of them, and they were very excited about their vacation. This work event was their last stop before they would leave.

Well, as everyone broke apart from the prayer circle, I made my way to her.

"Hey, I was wondering if I could pray for you. I feel like God was highlighting you during the prayer time, and I'm supposed to pray for you and your immediate family."

I didn't know her church background or how she felt about strangers approaching her regarding personal prayer. I can imagine one might have reservations about that. So, her initial response was to say that maybe it was for her sister, as she gestured towards her sister standing close by. I took in the suggestion and looked at her sister as I waited and listened for a moment while checking in with Holy Spirit. He made it clear that it was not for her sister that I was to pray for, but again it was for her and her immediate family.

The awkwardness grew a little as I told her what I felt, and she finally agreed and allowed me to pray for her and her immediate family. So, I started to pray and leaned into the Holy Spirit for the right word for protection for all. I remember it wasn't a long prayer full of impressive words. It was just a simple little prayer spoken in faith.

Once done, as the crowd thinned out, we left too. Almost immediately after we stepped out of the door, I started to come down on myself hard, thinking, "Did I hear God right? Ugh, I'm such an idiot! Why do I always have to be so awkward? Can't I just be normal? I bet she thinks I'm such a weirdo!" While jumping into the car, I just recall feeling bad about myself. Picking up on the way I was feeling, my mentor and friend advised me not to worry too much about it and that I was really overthinking it. At the time, that was easier said than done, as the heaviness was coming down on me hard, but I was going to give it the good old college try as we pulled out of the parking lot together and left.

Four days later, I got a call from my friend who had been with me at the event. She said that she'd got a call from the lady I prayed for during the meet-up. The lady had called her and said she was looking for me and asked for my number. As far as I knew, the lady was currently enjoying the sea and sun with her sister on the cruise. So, I was totally confused as to why she would be calling around looking for me, of all people. My friend had called me first to give me a heads-up that she would be calling me and that it was about something big. For the life of me, I could not have guessed what I was about to hear.

A few moments later, the phone rang again – it was the lady herself. "Don't hang up! Don't hang up!" she cried between sobs. I waited patiently on the line for probably five minutes before she was able to catch her breath enough to start putting sentences together.

She said that she was on her way home with her sister from the ship because, while already on board, she got the most disturbing call from her husband. Their daughter was driving home on the way back from college when she got into a huge car accident with a transport truck that crashed into her. Her daughter's car had been totally wrecked. The police and emergency workers said she should have been killed, but praise God; it was a total miracle that she was alive and only walked away with a few minor scrapes and bruises.

The woman was beyond thankful that I had been obedient to the leading of the Lord just a few short days before. She asked if we could get together the following week as she wanted to thank me in person, and we met the following week. I thank God for what He had done for her and her family that day and how He protected them. We serve an awesome God indeed!

WHAT'S WITH THE WORD NATION?

About two years before I became a mom, I was having this experience for about two weeks - I would often hear the word "Nation." And every single time I heard it, I would have a noticeable physical reaction; something in the core of me would "move." Finally, after two weeks of wondering, I decided, hey, why don't I just ask God about this! It clearly wasn't going away. So that's what I did one afternoon while at church. I was walking down the long hallway when I casually asked the Lord, "So, what's with the word 'Nation?'" Without hesitation, as if He was waiting for me to ask, He replied, "That's your daughter's name!"

I stopped dead in my tracks! "Omigosh, Lord, that's brilliant! I love that name!" I thought back in reply. It was just perfect, and I would never have thought of that one on my own. Nor would I have guessed in a million years that this word was going to be the name of my future daughter. I was in love with it already! I have never personally heard of it as being someone's name. That was until I was listening to the audio

Bible, the book Matthew, chapter 1, listing off the genealogy of Jesus. As it turns out, "Nation" is actually the name of King David's great, great, great, great grandfather, spelled *Nahshon*. This was all very exciting!

Jeremiah 29:11 says, *"For I know the plan I have for you,"* declares the LORD, *"plans to prosper you and not to harm you, plans to give you hope and a future."* At the time, I was months away from tying the knot with my fiancé. We were both excited about starting a family and becoming parents, so it was all super exciting to hear about these plans God had for us. Fast-forward about eighteen months and we were expecting our first child, who, as you guessed, is a girl! We couldn't wait to see and hold our precious little Nation for the first time. And to this day, every time I hear her name, I can't help but smile on the inside.

Chapter 4

Healing

Healing is such an important part of the conversation when understanding salvation and what GOD has done for us through His Son Jesus on the cross.

The bottom line is that God wants you to be well: spirit, soul, and body. Not just some part of you or even the part of you that will live on in the sweet by and by. No, He wants all of you to be well, yesterday, today, and forever!

But first, if we are going to talk about healing and health, let's chat a little about the background of sickness and disease. Where did sickness come from in the first place, and how did God respond to it? I'm going to take my time with this one and lay it on thick for you because it's a good thing to grasp this topic as God intended.

So, to answer the first question, how did sickness and disease all start, we need to go back to the beginning of Adam and Eve. You see, they ended up believing a lie about themselves in the Garden of Eden that got the sickness and disease ball rolling.

One day as Adam and Eve were enjoying the good life in the Garden, the now-defeated Satan approached them with his shady self and got to work. He started off by casually asking, "Eve, did God really say you can't eat any of the fruit in the garden?" Obviously, he knew that was a lie and just wanted to pull her into a conversation. Here's a great lesson right off the bat: some conversations are not worth entertaining or getting into. Don't waste your time getting baited.

Eve replied to the serpent, "No, that's not true; we can eat the fruit from the trees in the garden, just not from the tree in the middle, or else we shall surely die!" (Gen 3:3)

The now-defeated Satan then moved into phase two of his plan and said, "That's a flat-out lie! You will not die. As a matter of fact, the instant you eat it, you will become just like God, and you will be able to tell the difference between good and evil – and He knows it!"

Eve took a second look at the tree, and suddenly, it looked a little different to her – juicier and more desirable – and she was in! She remarked to the serpent how she wanted more wisdom anyway and threw caution to the wind and took her first bite.

Where does wisdom come from? God says in James 1:5, *"If any of you lacks wisdom you should ask God and God will generously give to all without finding fault and it shall be given."* Even if you are in search of more wisdom, you don't have to go at it alone; just simply ask for it, and God's got you covered. If Eve felt like she was in need in the wisdom department, she could have easily had that conversation with God, and He would have been more than happy to help!

From there, she shared the fruit with her husband, Adam, and in that very moment they both became aware that there was good and there was evil. These two things were brand new to them, Good and Evil. Before that, all they had known was The Best!

Now suddenly, standing there naked, just as they always had been, they became painfully aware of a different kind of reality, a foreign emotion that they had not known before shame! Up until that point, they had lived their whole lives in innocence, in a place of total abundance on every level with nothing missing, nothing broken. Then to their surprise despite being pre-warned by God, they were now conscious of being naked in a new kind of way and the humiliation of it.

Being naked didn't come with the freedom they once had, and their first act of being more "knowledgeable" was to hide themselves and cover-up out of the shame of being exposed. They didn't do such a bang-up job of it either, by using fig leaves to hide their parts. Right from the word "Go," they were trying to fix what they had broken with their own resources without the help of God. This is referred to as the do-it-yourself system. This was the very thing that defeated Satan used to entrap them. He offered them a do-it-yourself solution to become more like God. But even so, God, in His love and mercy, stepped in to help them out. "The Lord God made garments of skin for Adam and his wife and clothed them" (Genesis 3:21). Not because He needed them to cover up for His sake, but because He saw the anguish and guilt they were going through. So, he killed the first animal and covered them up better than what they came up with on their own. From the very start of the Bible, you can see that the prophetic picture of pointing to Jesus dying on the cross and being a covering for mankind starts rolling in early on after the fall of man. You see it with this very act of God stepping in to cover them.

Although Adam and Eve were made in the image of God, immediately after they decided to eat the fruit that God told them not to eat in the first place, things started to change. Separation from God had begun.

Remember when Eve said to the serpent, "If we eat from that tree, we shall surely die"? This is that death she was referring to without even fully understanding what she was saying. God is the source of all life, and being separated from Him on any level brings about a sort of death. But why and how is that even possible?

Well, first off, the whole point of them eating the fruit was to gain something; they seemed completely oblivious to the fact that they already had everything in the first place.

Listen, on your worst day, you can have God plus nothing, and it would still equal EVERYTHING! How much truer was that for Adam and Eve in their innocence before the fall! And so, by way of defeated Satan's innuendos, they believed that they were lacking and needed something "more." There is where they believed the lie about themselves that led them into separation, sin, and death.

The fundamental truth is that knowing what God says about you and believing it, matters! A lot! It can be life or death. Once you believe what God says about you to be true, you can dismiss anything contrary.

Because Adam and Eve already had the very best during their time in Eden, and because God is a good, loving Father, He still wanted to provide them with a choice. God is not a "forcing" God; He's not into forcing people into loving Him. That wouldn't be love at all now, would it? For God IS love, and He's all about authentic relationships, not dictatorship.

The tree was there in the first place to offer a choice. What choice could they possibly have had as an option when they already had everything in the Garden? The only choice left to offer was something outside of their relationship with God and their total dependence on Him.

The only thing left was a do-it-yourself way of living and a dependency on themselves instead of the already secure dependency they had on God. Remember, everything was free before they ate the fruit, but after they were chased out of the Garden, they had to work and sweat for the bare minimum just to get by until the day they died. Such a contrast to Eden!

All that was left to offer as a choice was a "lesser" reality and all that it involves. That became available to them in the form of the low-hanging fruit on a tree called "The Tree of Knowledge of Good and Evil."

I mean, if you ask me, God had made it super easy. "I need to give them a choice," He might have thought, "but I'll only give them just one. That way, it shouldn't be too hard to obey my commandment of 'Don't touch!'"

It's not like they were tempted with a hundred or even ten trees out of all the millions of trees they had full access to. Only one tree!

The truth, however, is, even if God is trying to help us, it's still up to us to believe that He has our best interests at heart and to obey. We still get to choose in the end, and sometimes we make the wrong one.

Being shamefully aware of their nakedness, unfortunately, was just the beginning of that experience of separation. Now that they had come out from under God's set-up, they were living a new reality outside of union with God. From that day, through them, death was introduced to the world, and that included pain, sickness, disease, hardship, hatred, depression, jealousy, disaster, and more. Even so, they were so infused with the life of God before the fall that it took Adam 930 years to die physically. He probably still looked like he was 25 at the age of 323. As a side note, I wouldn't be surprised if we start seeing the average life expectancy increase as we continue to see an increase in the glory of God manifested around the world as promised.

But even still more, because of God's immeasurable love and mercy towards us, He wasn't willing to just leave us in that broken state. He already had a plan in place for mankind even before we even knew we needed one. His plan was to restore us to His original union, image, and likeness of Him, just like Adam and Eve experienced in the Garden. God's merciful plan came in the form of a Person, and that person was His Son, Jesus!

Fast forward many generations and biblical prophecies later (basically, conversations that God has had with man, letting them know that a Savior is coming), and we thankfully end up with an amazing Grand finale to this very lengthy prophetic conversation God had with mankind throughout the entire

Old Testament. Jesus dying on a cross! Jesus came as a sacrifice in payment for the sins of the world. For with God, things are free and life giving but, with the now-defeated Satan and sin, everything comes at a cost. Sin is a hard taskmaster that has no mercy, and it will come to collect! The payment for our sins is death!

Jesus came to pay our debt for us, not because we asked Him to because we didn't even know the full extent of our transgression and how much we really needed a Savior. Furthermore, to add insult to injury, when He came, He was treated like garbage, yet He still went to the cross willingly and, might I add, joyously.

Because of the joy awaiting him, he endured the cross, disregarding its shame. Now he is seated in the place of honor beside God's throne (Hebrews 12:2 NLT).

Jesus did for us what we couldn't do for ourselves. He became a man like us, so He could represent us, die for us, and set us free. A man acquired the debt, and a man had to pay it; only none of us qualified because the man who paid had to be blameless. None of us would like to pay the debt for another if we were innocent, but Jesus happily volunteered for the job for our sake and was born just like a man to fulfill the Father's plan of redemption.

For as in Adam all die, so in Christ all will be made alive (1 Corinthians 15:22).

Jesus' sacrifice on the cross was the atonement for our sins, which means coving over someone's debt. Prior to Jesus' sacrifice, the Israelites would have an annual sacrificing ritual on the Day of Atonement. The high priest would sacrifice an animal, and its blood would be sprinkled on the altar in payment for his sins and the sins of the nation; then, the slate would be wiped clean (Leviticus 16). However, this ritual had to be enacted yearly, for the shelf life of this sacrifice was only good for 365 days before it would expire, and then they would have to do it all over again. It was a band-aid solution to an infected cut that just wouldn't heal. Here we see the do-it-yourself system in action again, and like always, it falls short.

But Jesus' sacrifice on the cross was a one-time act, powerful enough to make provision to save, heal, and deliver all of mankind, past, present and future, the first time around. There would be no other sacrifice or payment needed ever again. Our sin was nailed to the cross with Him. He went down to the grave and left sin there, then came back up with a new life.

He didn't put a band-aid on our sin and fallen state or stitch it up to try and fix it. You are not a "reformed" creature in Christ. He got rid of the old model and started afresh with a new one. You are a completely brand spanking new creation in Christ!

Here's an amazing scripture from 2 Corinthians 5:17 *"Therefore if any man be in Christ, he is a new creature: old things are passed away; behold all things are become new."*

But did you know it wasn't just Jesus who died on the cross? You were up there with Him, too (Romans 6:6). Not up there with Him like the guy to the right or to the left of Jesus. Nope, you were hanging up there with Jesus on His cross, being co-crucified with Him, and as far as God is concerned, that means that you have overcome sin and the effects it used to have on your life, sickness being one of them.

Sickness is not a by-product of life: it's a direct result of the events that took place in the garden according to the bible. But now, sin has been dealt with on the cross. Sickness is part of the curse of death, for the wages of sin is death (Romans 6:23). But since our sin has been canceled on the cross, we don't have to live with death or sickness. Yes, we will one day die just as one day we were born. But, for the time being, we don't have to live a life of sickness as part of our portion any longer; rather, health can be our portion as far as the bible is concerned.

Romans 6 is an awesome chapter in the bible. It drives the point home that you are free from sin and all its side effects. I would highly recommend spending some personal time getting this into your heart and mind, so it becomes a permanent fixture in your spirit. But, for now, I have highlighted some points in the Mirror Bible translation of Romans 6, specifically verses 5 to 23. Check it out.

Verse 5: *We were like seeds planted together in the same soil, to be co-quickened to life. If we were included in his death we are equally included in his resurrection.*

Verse 6: *We perceive that our old lifestyle was co-crucified together with him; this concludes that the vehicle that accommodated sin in us was scrapped and rendered entirely useless. Our slavery to sin has come to an end.*

Verse 7: *If nothing else stops you from doing something wrong, death certainly does.*

The problem is that some of us don't believe this; therefore, sin is still a big part of the picture in our life. We are either dead to sin, or we're not; it's impossible to be both. How can you be dead and alive all at the same time? Not to mention many still have more faith in what Adam did in the Garden than what Jesus accomplished on the Cross. Renewing your mind and remembering daily what Jesus did will help. Meditate on the good news reality often, and you'll see a significant shift in your thoughts. This is important because as a man thinks, so is he!

Verse 9: *It is plain for ALL to see that death lost its dominion over Christ in his resurrection; he need not ever die again to prove a further point.*

Verse 10: *The reason for his death was to take away the sin of the world.*

Verse 11: (You'll like this one, I know it!) *This reasoning is equally relevant to you. Calculate the cross; there can only be one logical conclusion; he died your death; that means you died to sin and are now alive to God. Sin-consciousness can never again feature in your future! You are in Christ Jesus; his Lordship is the authority of this union.*

Verse 12: *You are under no obligation to sin; it has no further rights to dominate your dead declared body. Therefore, let it not entice you to obey its lusts.*

Verse 14: *Sin was your master while the law was your measure; now grace rules.*

Verse 15: *Being under grace and not the law most certainly does not mean that you now have a license to sin.*

You are not free to sin now all you want – that's not what this chapter is saying at all, in case anyone is confused. If anything, it's saying you are free to never sin again if you really understand what took place on the cross.

But, Melissa, what about the part in the bible where it says every man has sinned and has fallen short? Well, yes, I don't deny it; that's the whole point, the reason why we needed a Saviour, in Jesus in the first place. Because sin has touched every man because of Adam, how much more has righteousness touched us because of Jesus? The Christian life doesn't have to be a yo-yo one. One day you're up and awesome, and the next day down in the dumps giving yourself over to the "sin life" like you have no control. Quite the opposite. God has not given you a spirit of fear but of love, power, and a sound mind. Go ahead and use it! (2 Timothy 1:7)

Verse 18: *Sin once called the shots; now righteousness rules.*

Woohoo, thank you, Jesus!

Verse 22: *Consider your life now; there are no outstanding debts; you owe sin nothing!*

Verse 23: *…the reward of the law is death; the gift of grace is life! The bottom line is this; sin employs you like a soldier for its cause and rewards you with death; God gifts you with the highest quality of life all wrapped up in Christ Jesus our Leader.*

You see, it's so clear. Instead of getting a bill statement like we should have gotten for our sin saying, "We owe," we ended up with a receipt saying, "PAID IN FULL!" You are free, and whom the Son sets free is free indeed. Not only that. but now the Lord is the Spirit, and where the Spirit of the Lord is, there is freedom (2 Corinthians 3:17). Does the Holy Spirit not live in us, and are we not the temples of the Holy Ghost? If that is true and if where the Spirit of the Lord is, there is freedom and if you can find Him in us, then we can conclude that we have freedom. Part of the freedom that God is talking about includes freedom from sickness. So, what else did the cross and the payment Jesus made cover for us anyway? Isaiah 53:4-5, foretold the purpose of the cross perfectly, *It was our pains he carried – our disfigurements, all the things wrong with us. We thought he brought it on himself, that God was punishing him for his own failures. But it was our sins that did that to him, that ripped and tore and crushed him - our sins! He took the punishment, and that made us whole. Through his bruises we get healed* (MSG).

To recap, one of the main reasons for the cross was to make us whole, to get us healed!

The above scripture is in the Old Testament and is talking about a future event on the cross that had not yet happened at that time. But the next one below found in the New Testament is referring to a past one after the cross: 1 Peter 2:24: *By his stripes you were healed*!

You see, on this side of the cross, healing has been pre-paid as far as God is concerned; sin and sickness have no more power over you. You were healed! The last words that Jesus spoke before He gave Himself up to death were, "It is finished!" The chains were broken that day, and the veil was torn. The separation created in the Garden and the division it caused between Man and God is no more.

The fact is before the fall, Adam and Eve weren't sick a day in their lives in the Garden. I would bet they didn't even have a cough or cold ever! How much better should it be for us now that the veil is torn and the Holy Spirit lives in us! (John 14:16-17)

David says it beautifully in Psalm 103:1-5,

Praise the LORD, my soul! Praise his holy name, all that is within me. Praise the LORD, my soul, and never forget all the good he has done: He is the one who forgives all your sins, the one who heals all your diseases, the one who rescues your life from the pit, the one who crowns you with mercy and compassion, the one who fills your life with blessings so that you become young again like an eagle(GWT).

I love how David says, "Never forget"! For me, that scripture goes hand and hand with Romans 12:2 that says, "Renew your mind daily!" What does that mean? It means to remember every single day what GOD has given you. He has healed all your diseases; He has redeemed your life from destruction and blessed you with all the other benefits that come with the free gift God has given us wrapped up in His Son Jesus.

The fact is healing is the Children's Bread (Matthew 15:26). If you are saved, then you are a child of God and therefore have the right to the inheritance that was bequeathed to you when Jesus died (John 1:12). Healing and health are part of that inheritance.

Once a woman in a wheelchair approached me for prayer, and I asked her what she wanted prayer for, and she replied, "I want to walk!" Before we started to pray for her to walk again, I led her through a prayer of repentance and salvation. I did that because I know that healing is the children's bread, the children's blood-bought benefit. Once I knew that she was saved, it was easy to pray for her to walk as it was her right. So, instead of praying from a place of begging, I prayed from a place of expecting. It's always good to pray from a place of expecting, but how much more when you are a child of God and healing is not a luxury for just a few: it's a right for all God's children!

This is not to say that God can't heal someone who has not given their life over to Him. The bible says, "God healed ALL who came to Him" (Luke 9:11; Matthew 12:15; Acts 10:38). I'm sure He got a good mix of everyone in the "all." Neither is this a two-step formula on how to pray and heal the sick. God doesn't want you to rely on formulas – He wants you to rely on Him. EVERY SINGLE TIME!

How someone receives their healing one way can be totally different from how another person receives their healing. In the bible you have examples of blind eyes being opened through different methods. For one man, Jesus spits on the ground first to make mud and then puts it on the man's eyes, telling him to go dip in the pool of Siloam, afterwards to wash it off and then he would be able to see (John 9:6-7). But He didn't repeat this same formula for another man. Jesus changed it

every time. Even still, sometimes, you will pray more than once for the same healing. Jesus prayed more than once in Mark 8:22-25 over another blind man. The first time, he was partially healed. Then Jesus prayed a second time, and this time, he was totally healed. Don't get stuck in a pattern or in the way of doing things: God will surprise you.

There is, however, one thing I would remain consistent in through any sort of healing. John G. Lake, who had hundreds of thousands of healing testimonies under his ministry, said it like this: "It is not TRY but TRUST...This is the secret of Christ's healing; that is the secret of Christ's salvation. It is trusting Him for it and believing Him when He says, He will do it, and the mind relaxes, and the soul comes into rest" (John G. Lake). "Trust is Faith, and Faith looks like rest!" Lake continued.

Jesus Himself was having a nap in the middle of a storm on the sea (Mark 4:38-40). His disciples were in a complete panic, crying out, "Master, do you want us to drown? Wake up!" Jesus woke up, and with one small sentence, commanded the wind to stop. And it did. When storms and trouble come your way, our souls should and need to be at rest. If they are not, start with renewing your mind daily, and remember who you are in Christ because of Christ! Also make sure to do this even when you are not standing smack dab in the middle of a storm. Do it on sunny days as well. It will help greatly if and when you are feeling the winds start to kick up. Renew your mind daily regardless of the rain or shine.

Remember, as Jesus said, your heavenly Father only gives you good things:

"Which of you, if your son asks for bread, will give him a stone? Or if he asks for a fish, will give him a snake? So you who are evil know how to give good gifts to your children, how much more your Father in heaven will give good things to those who ask Him!" (Matthew 7:9-11)

Isn't healing and good health included among those good things? Not only is it included, but if you ask me, it's right up there at the top of the list, along with salvation!

God has already done the heavy lifting here, guys. Our small part in the matter is to simply trust and believe. Like that forbidden tree in the Garden of Eden, God is not making it too complicated for us. Even still, I know for some, this sounds really hard, but that's because you are relying on yourselves to drum up some faith. But you don't have to. Even that part of the equation God took care of for us to make it easy.

How good of a God do we have that not only did He take care of His part but also helped us big time with ours: the believing/faith part! He knew that it would take trust and faith on our part, but He also knows how delicate humans can be, so again He made it really easy for us. Instead of us trying to muster up the faith to believe, He literally handed that to us on a silver platter and said, "Here you go!" According to Romans 12:3, God has given every believer *"the measure of faith"* (KJV).

When you think in terms of the amount of the "measure" that God has given to you personally, it's important not to minimize it, as if it's not enough. Even if He happened to give you the smallest amount, the size of a mustard seed, let's say, it would still be big enough to move a mountain. When God gives, He does it generously, and that includes the measure of faith He has already given you as well (Matthew 17:20).

What would happen if you actually started believing that? What miracles and healings would you see take place? I hear Christians say all the time, "God, give me faith to believe. If only I had faith, this or that would happen." But what if we started using the faith we have already been given and go from there?

As I'm wrapping up this look at healing and giving you guys just a simple foundation for it, I will say I believe that the day is coming when we will see once again, as the knowledge and the glory of the Lord continues to cover and rise over the earth like the water covers the sea, hospitals and hospital beds being emptied – just like in 1918 in Spokane Washington with John. G. Lake and his ministries helped to accomplish this by praying for the sick in Jesus' name. With over one hundred thousand reported healings by the power of God and confirmed by doctors, it was arguably the healthiest city in the United States at the time. That was a lot of people back then. I mean that would still be a lot of people now. This is something that as a world would be amazing to see. The power of God doesn't have restrictions or know boundaries; it can travel far and wide and enter ICUs and hospital rooms too. I pray all of them would be flooded by it.

And now, some final thoughts. If you are on medication for something, I'm not here to tell you to stop taking it; that's between you, God, and your doctor. There are some amazing doctors that God uses, too, and medications that have helped people and brought about healing. Heck, even I take Tylenol if I have pain or a headache and have used the health system like anyone else at times. But what I'm saying is this: while you may be on medication, you have it within your right as a child of God to believe for your healing and health, no matter how big or small the healing need might seem. And as you believe, I believe you will see it come to pass for your life and for others around you.

Some people have been given a bad report with no help available from the medical system or a cure in sight. But with God, all things are possible. I also believe that it's important to use wisdom in everything and do the right things like exercising and keeping to a balanced diet with the right foods. It's not wise to sit in front of your TV and eat only donuts, right? Chances are you won't feel very good if you do. If you are having trouble in any area of health, lean into God for help and direction as well, for His grace is sufficient.

And, lastly, I want to leave you with a list of healing scriptures and stories to check out when you have a chance. They are so inspiring and faith stirring.

John 11:1-44: Jesus raises Lazarus from the dead.
Mark 2:9-12: Jesus heals the crippled man
Acts 5:15: Peter's shadow heals the sick as they are laid in the street, and he walks by them.
Luke 8:43-48: Jesus heals the woman with the issue of blood
John 4:46-47: Jesus cures the nobleman's son

Chapter 5

Radical Encounters and Testimonies Part II

RUN!

My family and I lived in Ottawa, Ontario, for a while and attended a lively, dynamic Jesus-believing church. We were leaders of the intercessory team there for a few years. Being a part of the leadership team, we would also minister to people who wanted prayer and ministry during the Sunday morning altar calls as well.

This Sunday, the altar up at the front was jam-packed with people coming up for prayer, and all the ministry team members were busy praying for people. I had just finished praying for someone with a line of people behind her waiting for me to pray for them too. When I looked up to see who might be next in line, I saw a lady in a wheelchair waiting for me – the woman I mentioned earlier. My first thought was, "Okay, who else is available to pray for her?" I looked to the left and the right, but no one was free. For a moment, I doubted myself to believe in this lady's healing. I saw the wheelchair and, for a split second, put more faith in the problem than in the promise. Then I quickly remembered it was not me that paid the price for her healing in the first place: it was Jesus – it had nothing to do with me, anyway. I was just the "blessed" one that He chose to work through, and I got to have a front, up close and personal seat, as I watched His amazing miraculous healing power at work! There was no pressure on me to heal her; I just believed Jesus already had at the cross, and I was expecting a miracle because of that.

While walking up to her, I had renewed my mind and thinking, and now I was totally ready and excited to pray for her! "Hello," I said, "What would you like me to pray for?" She looked at me with hope, "I want to walk!" I smiled big and said, "Great, let's shoot for that!"

Funny enough, I had just finished reading a book called *Azusa Street: They Told Me Their Stories* by J. Edward Morris. It was about the amazing testimonies that took place during the Azusa Street revivals back in 1906, led by Rev. William. J. Seymour. They would line up the people in wheelchairs often by the dozen in the same section together, and, one by one, they would all get up and walk when the word was spoken. But one of the things I had learned from Rev. Seymour in that book was that, if you are going to pray for someone in a wheelchair, first things first, move their foot pedals out of the way. It's an act of faith, for faith without works is dead. The moving of the pedals from down to up was the initial "works." If you really think that they will get up and walk, move them from the start, and make it so that they have no obstruction in their way *when* they take their first step. You see, it doesn't become a question of "if" but "when" they take their first step!

So that's what I did first. I moved her pedals up and out of the way. The second thing I did was lead her into a prayer of salvation. I did this because I didn't want to have any doubt that she was saved, and then if saved, she had all right to the healing power of God as a child of God (John 1:12). Not that this is a formula or that I do this every time before I pray for someone, but in this case, I also felt led to do so. After we finished the salvation prayer, I prayed for her healing. The only other thing left to do now was for her to get up and walk.

I couldn't help but think about Peter in Acts 3:7. It was not until he took the lame man's hand and helped him up that strength came into the man's legs, and he was healed. I believed that, as she started to stand, she would feel a change in her body too. I looked around, and the altar was starting to clear a bit, so I called for a few nearby people to come and help support her on either side while she attempted to stand, and we continued praying.

Then I held her hands out front to help pull her up. Next thing I know, she was standing up and started to put one foot in front of the other. She was slow and shaky, but she was doing it! She was starting to walk! Still, with the help of a few of us around her, she was probably on her fourth or fifth step when I heard the Lord say, "Stop and let go of her." So, I instructed everyone to take their hands off her and step back. Then I heard the Lord say, "Now tell her to RUN!" with major emphasis and volume on the word Run. "Wait! What? Are you sure, God, because I'm not sure if You noticed, but she's barely making steps on her own? And now You want me to tell her to RUN?"

I took a minute out to confirm this because I wanted to check-in. This was only the second person I had ever prayed for who was in a wheelchair, and I think it's okay to check with Holy Spirit as you are leaning on Him to lead you. But isn't it so like God to take a person who is barely standing or walking and then telling them to RUN? "Okay, God, if You say so."

So, I got really close to her and in a kind of whisper yelled (you know, like when kids think that they are whispering but everyone around them can still hear them?) "RUNNNNNN!"

At this point, I hadn't realized it, I was too caught up in what I was doing, but the whole church now had eyes upfront and were watching this scene. Immediately after I finished saying "RUN," it was like a bolt of lightning came down and struck her in an instant. The power of God shot right through her, and she literally took off running. She ran straight out the double doors of the sanctuary and into the hallway!

There must have been 300 to 400 hundred people there that day, and most of them jumped up and ran after her too. Now, praising God, surrounded by everyone in the hallway, this precious lady was just shouting and jumping with great joy, saying repeatedly, "Jesus loves you; Jesus loves you," and giving Him all the glory. The people joined in! What an amazing sight! She had come to church that day in a wheelchair, but she left on foot because of the faithfulness, love, and power of God.

I didn't know her personally, and I had no idea why she was in a wheelchair in the first place or the circumstances around it, but the following Sunday, a friend of hers brought me her doctor's letter as evidence, saying that she had been his patient for about ten years. Within that time, he had never seen her without a wheelchair due to multiple sclerosis until a few days ago when she walked into his office for the first time ever on her own two feet!

She had been in the chair for ten years, and within ten minutes, because of God, she was out. What God has done for this lady He can do for another, for He is the same yesterday, today, and forever! All glory, honor, and praise to God!

SO, THINK ABOUT IT!

It was late into the evening on October 20, 2011. My husband and I were already in bed. He had hit the pillow and was out like a light. I wasn't quite as tired yet, and I was still awake when suddenly, I heard God say to me: "So…think about it, but if you want, and if you do something about it today, you'll have a baby!"

Okay, first off, can we just break this down for a second? Here comes God Almighty, the Alpha, and Omega, the Creator of the whole Cosmos and Universe, and just said these words to me, "So…think about it."

I mean, who knew God even spoke that way, right? and, second, you mean to tell me He wants my input for something? That's amazing and insane all at the same time. I know God is all about relationships, but to sit back and hang out like we are "shooting the breeze" just talking about life choices over here has gotten me all fired up with some serious awe and wonder! Obviously, God is God and can do and say what He likes however He pleases, but often, we are taught in the church and some groups that there are layers, protocols, and procedures to having a conversation with God.

Coming boldly to the throne room of God is quoted often and spoken about in theory, but not always peeled back and looked at for what it is. "Coming boldly" is more about having 24-7 access to God and being confident that you can just go to God anytime you like – no appointment necessary, no pastor or priest to give you the A-Okay, all clear status. How is that possible? Because Jesus already did that when He died on the cross, and the veil between us was torn.

But, even still, I had never quite had a conversation with God on such a casual note like this one. Neither had I ever heard of someone else who did. I'm sure there are people out there who can raise a hand and testify that they have, but for me, I have never personally heard of it in my ten years of attending church and conferences up until that point.

Usually, we hear things like, "God told me to do this or that, or I feel like God is calling me to move here or go there." That is sometimes said in a somber tone. Yet, we never really hear about God coming to hang out with us and process a decision with us, do we? Yet, once I started thinking about it, I then realized He does and has, and it's in the bible too.

God is not a tyrant here or a harsh dictator – that's Satan's playground. Of course, there are times when God gives us instruction and direction, but He also wants to work together with us, and even at times, He completely stands back to see what we want to personally do and or come up with.

Let's take Adam, for example, one of his first jobs ever was to name the animals. God just sat back and gave him free rein, and you know what? I think he did a pretty good job at it too! Thousands of years later, and we still use the names he chose way back when. When I think about it, he could have named the animals: thing one, thing two, thing three, and so on. But he got really into it instead and came up with some amazing names.

When Adam was done, I can picture God taking it all in, standing back and saying something like, "On the hundredth day (or whatever day it may have been), all the animals have officially been named, and it was good!" You know how God does it.

The other amazing part about what God said to me was, "If you do something about it today…" Today! Here I had a timeframe. That also struck me as interesting. God gave me some important information that I needed to help make a decision. I didn't mind the short notice because, in the end, it wasn't a hard decision at all.

To give a little background, at the time, we already had two kids, and we always wanted a third. But our home was small, with only two bedrooms, and we wanted to wait until we got into a bigger home with more space for the family. So, we put it on the shelf for a later date. However, when God comes to you personally and asks if you want to be the mother of a precious little baby that He has in mind for you, you don't say, "No thanks" or "Let me think." Or at least I didn't but even still, instead of telling me I had to have this baby or just waking up one day with a nice little "surprise," He was asking me if I wanted to. And that means so much to me, knowing that He cares about what I want, and even more than that, I felt cherished and included! I love that I'm included! We all are!

It didn't take long for me to decide. I was utterly honored that God even approached me to see if I wanted to mother this very special baby that He had in mind. My personal timeline or plans didn't matter. I absolutely wanted a thousand percent to say yes to what God wanted to give us.

I couldn't help but think about what this baby would become and how special he or she must be. But mostly, I felt totally humbled that God would choose me. It's simple in the end, and even though God gave us the free will to choose, I want to use my free will to say YES to everything God has for me and asks me to do. Writing this book is one of them.

God knew I would say yes all along. He knows the way I think and every part of me, but He still took the time to reason with me, which is so amazing!

God says to Israel in Isaiah 1:18, "Come now and let us reason together." God wanted to reason with them. He wanted to chat and consider and decide a thing together with them. He wanted to "think about it" with them. and so, the decision was made that night.

I can tell you that I started feeling very early signs of pregnancy within the next 24 hours. I was surprised at that because it would usually take a bit more time. I know exactly what the signs were; this being my third pregnancy, I was more aware. Also, I think God was so thrilled about it, too, and that caused me to be extra sensitive to it all.

There was never a doubt that I would get pregnant that day once I said yes to what God was offering me, but the change in my body that I could feel was just a sweet layer added to the whole gift.

JOHN 3:16

Now pregnant with baby #3 and having two kids under four, I was praying about the date of my third baby's arrival. My two kids were born on the 16th of the month. My first was two days early, and my second was a whole eight days late. The funny thing is my husband, and I were each born on the 11th of our respective birth-months, and to make it even more interesting, my third was due on the 11th too.

So, it was about halfway through the pregnancy when I was chatting with God and asking Him about the date of the third's birthday. In my heart, I wanted him to have the same date as our other two kids and be born on the 16th. After asking God about this, I heard the Lord say to me without hesitation, "John 3:16."

In an instant, I knew exactly what God was saying. He was indeed saying that all three kids would be born on the 16th day, and He used such a clever way to say it. With God, there can also be layers to a thing. So, I decided to dig a little deeper with the verse itself. Proverbs 25:2 says, "*It is the glory of God to conceal a matter and the glory of kings to search it out*" (BSB). God loves a good hide-and-seek game.

The key scripture John 3:16 probably gets quoted more than any other scripture in the bible: "*For God so loved the world that he gave his one and only Son, that whoever believes in him shall not perish but have eternal life.*" I can see why God so loves the world. He gave and gave big time and, for those that believe in His precious Son Jesus, they will have eternal life in return! How amazing God is!

And so, after meditating on this scripture, I decided to take it even further and look up what the numbers 3 and 16 represented biblically. Here's what I found.

The number 3 represents completeness, and the Trinity, the 3 in 1. We know that through Christ and the cross, we are complete in Him.

The number 16 represents love. We can clearly see that in John 3:16 and in 1 Corinthians 13:4-7, the love scripture is often quoted at the altar during wedding ceremonies. The scripture in and of itself has 16 nouns associated with it, 16 markers that you can use as a backdrop to help you respond in love if ever you need a reminder or options. It has also been said that 16 is associated with manifestations. God so loving the world and sending His only begotten Son Jesus because of that love was the manifestation of all manifestations known to mankind! The word became flesh as Jesus manifested as a man.

So here I was, a little over halfway pregnant, and I had my answer. My third beautiful baby would be born on the 16th. It was settled with my soul, and I had zero doubt about it so much so that on my next appointment, I asked the midwife if she was working on the 16th of his birth month, four months down the road, and she said she was of course. Her next question was, "Why did you ask?" "Because I will be giving birth on that day!" She laughed and said, "Alright, let's see."

This midwife had been in this practice for over twenty years. She said very few women could guess their due date way in advance, let alone know it for sure, especially with normal delivery and not a scheduled C-section, plus only being halfway through the process – it's far out there. I mean, I totally get it; it was hard to believe, but I wasn't trying to convince her. I was just letting her in the picture so she could plan.

I also started telling my friends and family what the Lord had told me as well. I did that, too, because I wanted to let those I love to stand back and watch God do exactly what He said He was going to do. The whole situation was a chance for others to get closer to God. Anything that will help people in their faith, I'm here for it.

And so, the remainder of my pregnancy time went by, and finally, we had arrived at the 16th day of his birth month. The phone calls and text messages started to pour in from early in the morning into the afternoon. Family and friends were excited to meet him too. "How are you feeling?" "Is he here yet?" "Any contractions? Have you started labor?"

I had to answer no to all these inquiries. Not much was happening yet.

4:00 pm comes around, then 5:00, then 6:00 with the text messages still rolling in, but they started to read differently. Maybe people didn't want me to feel bad or get my hopes up, which I can understand. "Maybe it will be tomorrow," I heard, or "It's really hard to plan these things out."

They were just trying to be encouraging, but I still replied with a smile, "Thank you, but I'll text you when it begins. The day is not over yet, and he's coming today, I have no doubt."

It was now just about 8:00 pm, and I had just finished putting my two beautiful babies to bed and was shutting their doors closed. With my hand still on the doorknob, I felt it! A contraction had hit me, and I knew it was GO time.

From the very onset of labor my contractions were three minutes apart. After about an hour and a half or so, I called my midwife and told her I was in labor. She stayed on the phone with me to time them and to "feel me out" to get a sense of how I was feeling and to hear how my voice sounded, which helps indicate the intensity of labor. Three-minute apart contractions are close in the labor world and usually mean that the intensity is ramped up, plus it's hard to talk through it. I was still talking while having them. She concluded that it might just be Braxton Hicks, a term for false labor, yet your body still uses it to help get you ready for real labor – kind of like a pre-game, if you will, or practice run. She suggested this because I didn't sound like a woman who was having contractions that close. I seemed a bit too calm for her, and I was managing them well so I could see where she was coming from; nevertheless, she thought it best to swing by my house and do a quick check-in.

It was now after 10:00 pm when the midwife arrived at my home. She came upstairs, peeked her head through the door of my room, took one look at me on my hands and knees, swaying back and forth, and said, "Oh, you are in labor! I'll be right back with my bag and stuff." She didn't even bother to bring it in the first time because she really didn't think it was time. But it was clear that somewhere between the phone call with her and her arrival, labor leveled up and became more intense.

Being so late in the day with less than a few hours left, a lot of people were still wondering with anticipation if he would be born on the 16th or not. Again, I was just as convinced as I was when God spoke John 3:16 over months prior. This little baby inside and I both knew he was coming on the 16th.

Just a short time later, at 11:27 pm on the 16th this little beautiful precious baby from Heaven was born into our family. We were so thrilled and overjoyed to finally meet and hold him for the first time. God has said it, and it had happened! I couldn't wait for his brother and sister to meet him when they woke up. My 3x16s were all under one roof, and my heart was full.

As he was laying there nestled in my arms, I turned to my midwife and said, "Do you remember that time in your office when I asked you if you would be working on this day?"

She gasped, and the look on her face said it all. "Oh my gosh, yes I do!" She was in total shock and awe at what the Lord had done and added that she would never forget our family or this beautiful story. And God knows, neither will I.

Chapter 6

Dreams and Visions

For as long as I can remember, I have been dreaming. Even at five years old, I recall staying overnight at my grandmother's house during the summer nights, and the evening sun was still beaming through the window as my grandmother was putting me to bed. Most kids would protest that it was not bedtime because it was not yet dark outside. But, for me, I remember at times being more than happy to go to bed because, in my mind, I was going to the "other" place. I was going to the other world as I saw it and it was a lot of fun. My dreams were very real, vivid, and detailed, and I would constantly remember them when I woke up, much like I do now.

The bible is a great place to start when it comes to learning about dreams and visions and how God uses them to communicate with us at times. After all, He is the author of both, and when it comes to dreams; our relationship with God doesn't need to pause between 11:00 pm and 7:00 am while we get our beauty sleep. Nor does it stop while we are going about our day doing "all the things."

From the great book called the bible, we can see that God will use the vehicle of dreams and visions to speak. Sometimes it's very much straight to the point as in Genesis 20 when God spoke to Abimelech, the king of Gerar, about sleeping with Sarah, Abraham's wife. That night God came to Abimelech in a dream and told him, "You are a dead man, for that woman you have taken is already married!" (NLT) – I mean, that didn't need much of an interpretation! "You touch her, you die!" Pretty straight to the point. Can't really get clearer than that.

Then there are other times where God speaks, and it can feel a bit like an unsolved riddle. We will perhaps need to do a little more digging or searching to get the interpretation. Take, for instance, Judges 7:13-15.

When Gideon came, behold, a man was relating a dream to his friend. And he said, "Behold, I had a dream; a loaf of barley bread was tumbling into the camp of Midian, and it came to the tent and struck it so that it fell and turned it upside down so that the tent collapsed." And his friend replied, "This is nothing other than the sword of Gideon the son of Joash, a man of Israel; God has handed over to him Midian and all the camp."

When Gideon heard the account of the dream and its interpretation, he bowed in worship. Then he returned to the camp of Israel and said, "Arise, for the Lord has handed over to you the camp of Midian!" (NASB)

You can see how God spoke in "code" via the dream. A friend interpreted it, and now they had the instruction and confidence to move forward and win the day! Sometimes, we can share a dream or vision with someone, especially if they have a strong gift of interpretation and understand that way.

Still, other times we need to press into the Holy Spirit for that insight.

I would add, however, when sharing a dream or vision with a friend, it's best to still process what they say in consultation with the Holy Spirit. You see, some people will give interpretations based on their own perceptions filtered through the lens through which they see God. For example, I know some people who will always take a dream or vision as a warning or something bad. You could share a dream that is actually good and amazing, but they will only see doom and gloom. Now I'm not saying God doesn't give warnings to people in dreams and visions, but if that's all you see all the time, you will have to ask yourself, "Is this really God trying to speak to me, or perhaps it's me who views God and the spirit realm through a cloudy, distorted lens for whatever reason." So please choose wisely who you share these things with. I believe that if God gives you a dream a lot of the time, He is more than happy to help you get understanding from it. He loves when we do that; it's one of His primary ways: *"In all thy getting get understanding"* (Proverbs 4:7 KJV). So be confident that when you take your dream or vision to God, He will give you what you need to understand it.

For me, whether I gain understanding through a friend, who can help me navigate, or by asking the Holy Spirit, who can be a friend to all, either way, I find that it's helpful for me to see it all laid out in front of me from different angles. I like to see the big picture and the finer details all at the same time.

When it comes to the not so obvious dreams or visions, I think sometimes God wants to see who is going to take the time to consider what He is saying and diligently seek understanding.

He doesn't always hand over His "pearls" so easily because He wants to give them to people who also place value on them and will put in the time to ponder, ask questions, and get excited about what He is saying. It's to those people that He will reveal some of the hidden things, too. *"It is the glory of God to conceal a matter; to search out a matter is the glory of kings"* (Proverbs 25:2). He wants His revelations to be cherished, not played with for five minutes, and then discarded in the bottom of the toy bin, like a kid who gets bored with his toys.

Likewise, I find that there is a training factor to it as well. Sometimes God wants to coach us in this area and gifting. You can see that with Jeremiah, where God brings him through, what I call "vision boot camp," where He would show him a thing, and then they would work it out together.

Here's an example.

The word of the LORD came to me: "What do you see, Jeremiah?" I see the branch of an almond tree," I replied. The LORD said to me, "You have seen correctly, for I am watching to see that my word is fulfilled." The word of the LORD came to me again: "What do you see?" "I see a pot that is boiling," I answered. "It is tilting towards us from the North." The LORD said to me, "From the north disaster will be poured out on all who live in the land. I am about to summon all the peoples of the northern kingdoms," declares the LORD (Jeremiah 1:11-14).

At first, when God called Jeremiah out as a Prophet for the Nations, Jeremiah was quick to disqualify himself and give God all the reasons why, *"Alas, Sovereign Lord… I do not know how to speak; I am too young"* (Jeremiah 1:6). But God took his hand, reassured him that He would be with him, and started to build him up in his calling. I'm sure after each lesson with God, Jeremiah's confidence increased in the very thing he was called to do. Legs are made for walking, but we still need to learn how to stand on them first. God understands that we might feel overwhelmed and/or unqualified to do the very thing we are called to do, so He comes alongside us and gives us what we need to help us grow in that very thing.

Visions can feel much like a dream, except the main difference is you are awake. While dreams come in the form of images and movie-like reels, visions can come in several different ways. My husband, for one, gets open visions that appear out of thin air in front of his face and have moving parts. One time he was standing in church worshipping, and suddenly, in front of him about face-high, these images appeared as if he was watching a movie or TV screen. He couldn't believe his eyes and even started to swat at it, to see if he was imagining. The image he was seeing was of a future event in his life. This kind of vision is rightfully named a panoramic vision, and I'm always in awe when I hear about this kind of vision being given to someone. It must be exciting to see with your natural eyes as it all unfolds in front of you.

My visions come more to me like an impression, a thought, or a feeling that I'm picking up about myself or someone. It usually comes like a snapshot or a still image or picture in my mind that might be accompanied by a feeling or a knowing. Recently, I felt the name "Benjamin" pop up in my spirit when I was speaking to someone over the phone who had a loved one who had just passed away. The name just appeared mid-conversation, so within myself, I asked the Holy Spirit for more information about Benjamin, and then I just had a knowing that the person Benjamin was a child. So, I asked this person, "Who is Benjamin? Is he someone's son?" I thought that it could have been her recently deceased friend's son since I got the impression while we were speaking of them. The person I was talking to had to think for a moment; it didn't come to her right away. After a moment, the lady eagerly said, "Yes, I know Benjamin! Benjamin was my friend's godson. Benjamin passed away as well, 10 years back.

See, sometimes when you think you have missed it, you haven't. I thought maybe I missed it because it took her a few minutes for her to confirm the word. God knows exactly what He is saying and how He wants to say it. And, if you do happen to miss it, say so and keep going. Get around people who are gifted in this area with whom you feel safe to practice and can comfortably share what you believe God is saying. You don't want to miss out on God using you to bless someone or to shy away from it because you missed something. *"Good words are honeycombs, and the sweetness thereof is a healing of the soul"* (Proverbs 16:24 BST).

The name I disclosed was really comforting to the lady in knowing that God would "go out of His way" to bring up such a detail. These are things that I could have never known. What are the odds that I would pick out the exact name that turned out to be the name of someone relevant for this situation? I mean how many millions and millions of names are there to pick one from? In His wisdom and love, God was saying that the two are now together again in paradise through their passing away. How comforting that would be not only to the person I was speaking to during such a difficult time but also to the biological parents of the little boy named Benjamin?

Remember when I said in Chapter 2 that a lot of these spiritual gifts tend to intertwine with each other? Well, this is one great example. I want to take a moment and break it down for you to help you understand how the Holy Spirit speaks to me sometimes so that you might recognize it in your own encounters with God.

The vision first started out and came to me in the form of a mental impression. I saw the name "Benjamin" appear in my thoughts in big, bold **letters.** From there, a layer of "knowing" was added to the word of knowledge after I pressed into Holy Spirit, asking if He could give me more details about Benjamin. And that's when I felt that Benjamin was a boy and possibly the son of the person we were discussing. Although it wasn't his biological son it turned out to be his godson. Still extremely relative and that's just sometimes how GOD works with us. Words of knowledge are a part of the prophetic family, but in this case, the word of knowledge came by way of a vision. And so, you can see how these things can easily tie together and overlap. Much like the body of Christ, the various members are not in competition with each other but instead are meant to work together in a harmonious way to bring about the will of God.

And since we are talking about dreams and visions, I wanted to touch on a popular scripture that is often quoted about visions and dreams. I didn't really understand it for the longest time:

Your sons and daughters will prophesy, your young men will see visions, your old men will dream dreams (Acts 2:17).

At a young age, I would experience all three – prophecy, visions, and dreams – and still do now. So one day, I just thought I'd ask God for some clarity on it. I'd thought I'd share with you, too, just in case you have ever wondered the same thing.

Here is what He said that if we look in the natural world, it's not common to see kids prophesying. The textbooks would say that such knowledge is not for kids –leave the spiritual matters in the hands of those they belong to.

Even Jeremiah, who God called out as prophet to the nations long before he was even formed in his mother's womb, responded with, "Sorry God – can't; too young!" According to man's standards, a lot of times, the consensus is that those things are best left in the hands of those with titles at the top of the religious ladder. Those are the ones that know the voice and will of God, right? Now, I'm not saying that those with positions and titles among the church organizations can't prophesy or hear the voice of God. We would hope for nothing less. Please, dear God, let the Church know your voice, if not anything else. But what is being added here is this: so can children.

Jesus was a huge fan of kids and still is. I daresay, He probably enjoyed being with them more at times than anyone else. Kids just have a natural, spontaneous faith that I know He loves so much! It would do us good to remember that child-like faith. However, oftentimes kids are dismissed and discounted in the church as not being old enough or qualified enough to hear the voice of God and prophecy.

Then we have the young men and women who see visions. This type of vision mentioned in this scripture, I believe, can be two-fold. Visions can refer to a supernatural experience, which some again believe are only for the "seasoned," that is, the "mature" believer who has climbed the invisible spiritual ladder amongst religious folks. But it also can refer to having a plan for your life, as in, "Write the vision and make it plain" (Habakkuk 2:2) scenario as you look ahead into your future and start making plans. Either way, most would think that an age requirement is necessary.

And, finally, old men (and women) will dream dreams. Old age in the natural world can often go hand in hand with not remembering things, let alone in a dream. But for God, these things are non-issues, for does not Psalm 77:11 say, *"But then I recall all you have done, O LORD; I remember your wonderful deeds of long ago"* (NLT)?

In the same way that old men will dream dreams and remember them, the wisdom of God will rest upon young men easily despite their lack of years, and kids will prophesy and clearly hear the voice of God even though they are only children. It's not by our human might nor by our power no matter how hard we try but rather something much better than any of that: "It's by My Spirit," says the Lord. (Zechariah 4:6)

Chapter 7

Radical Encounters and Testimonies Part III

GLORY BALLS

This is a very radical encounter that I had with the Lord. It started off as a dream encounter and then continued after I woke up. I have had a few encounters of this kind over the years where a dream continues when I am awake. This particular encounter is so remarkable I actually had a painting done by a professional realist artist so I could have it in my house to be reminded of it every day.

In my dream, I was in my living room, and Father God appeared. I knew it was the Father coming to me and not necessarily Jesus or Holy Spirit, even though they are all one. I believe that God intentionally came to me as Father God who art in Heaven, Holy is His name. Even though the three Persons in God are one, they have different attributes and different things to impart. Sometimes I feel the Holy Spirit, and other times I feel Jesus, specifically.

So, standing there in my home was the father, tall in stature and comforting as well. He was wearing a beautifully brilliant white robe. I did not see His face in detail as it was shining too brightly, but I did see Him in great detail from the neck down.

The Father was holding in His right hand this absolutely incredible, beautiful see-through sphere. The sphere was alive with an atmosphere of its own – this is the best way I can describe it. It had bright white clouds with lightning shooting from one place to another. I could hear rumbles of thunder. It was a storm of power that gave me the feeling it was coming straight out of the throne room of God! It was incredible to gaze upon!

I asked the Lord if I could hold it. As if He was just waiting for me to ask it, He said, "Yes, of course. As a matter of fact, you can have it to keep; not only that but here, take two." As He was saying that He stretched out His hands to give them to me, and He was now holding two glory balls instead of just one.

As I reached out to take hold of them, I started to get completely rocked under the power of God. The closer I got to them, the more I was becoming totally overwhelmed by the power of God and His splendor in these two orbs.

The next thing I knew, I was awakened out of the dream in mid-reach. The dream now crossed over to my waking moments, and the same feeling I had in the dream continued in the feeling I was experiencing while lying in my bed, now awake. I was completely overtaken and intoxicated by the power and love of God running through my whole body like waves of electricity. I felt completely drunk in the spirit, both in my dream as He was handing me the glory balls and now as I lay there awake in my bed.

There's a place in God where we become completely intoxicated by His love. One of my favorite scriptures speaks is of the beloved saying of her lover: "*Let him kiss me with the kisses of his mouth – for your love is more delightful than wine*" (Songs of Solomon 1:2). In other words, "Let Your love be the thing that I become so intimate with, for Your love is more influential than wine." In the same way that wine can influence you, God's love can intoxicate, and this is the intoxication that I was experiencing. You can drink till you're overflowing with zero side effects. God loves it when we drink in His love. "Have your fill!" He is saying.

After this encounter subsided, I went back to ponder the experience. I believe the Father was showing me that He wants to share all that He has and all that He is with us and used the glory balls to get the point across and place it into our hands.

The Father is always ready to give. He is marked by giving, and no one can outgive Him! Giving was His idea in the first place. He gave Adam and Eve the garden and everything they would need in it (Genesis 2). God so loved the world that He gave His only begotten Son (John 3:16). "*Don't not be afraid, little flock, for it gives your Father great happiness to give you the Kingdom,*" said Jesus (Luke 12:32 NKJV).

We celebrate Him who supercharges us powerfully from within. Our biggest request or most amazing dream cannot match the extravagance of His thoughts, who "*is able to do exceedingly abundantly above all we ask or think, according to the power that works in us"* (Ephesians 3:20 NKJV). In this encounter, I was just looking to have a peek at this amazing and powerful glory ball He was holding, and God's heart was to give it to me for keeps! Not only that but, true to Himself, He doubled it, giving me more than I asked for!

You, beloved, are on His mind and in His heart and thoughts. He comes with open arms and hands ready to give you His all so that you may experience His overwhelming, inebriating love with which He wants to fill you to the brim. It's just like His first miracle where Jesus instructed the servants to fill the water pots to the brim. I pray that you would receive the same from Him today.

ANGELS AND WINE!

My husband and I were treated to a beautiful dinner with some friends one night at one of the nicest restaurants we'd ever been to, and the meal was unforgettable! We all went together in one car. During the drive home, my husband and I, seated at the back, were talking about the supernatural and angels. This prompted my friend to start sharing about the time they were driving between states, and their car was on its last leg of gas, moments away from sputtering out. Praying they made it to a gas station before they got stranded, my friend suddenly sensed an angel close by and could see in her spirit the angel come up behind them and push their car forward until they got to a gas station as it was now running on E.

As we listened to her share this encounter, suddenly, I could sense the aroma of rich red wine as if someone had opened a bottle under my nose. I interrupted the conversation and asked if there was a bottle in the car that may have suddenly busted open or got smashed somehow, even though it had been a smooth drive on the highway for the last 20 minutes. But, no, there was no wine in the car. The strong aroma lasted for a few minutes and then was gone.

God gave us five senses, but it's not often that we hear of our sense of smell being aroused during a supernatural experience, maybe because we tend to naturally lean into sight or touch more. The only other time I ever learned about the scent being used in the supernatural in the church was the smell of sulfur, which we link to the demonic. Heavenly fragrance testimonies should outweigh all that. Can you imagine the different scents that must flood Heaven? Are we not seated in Heavenly places? God LOVES fragrance! The bible mentions scents and fragrances throughout: frankincense, myrrh, cinnamon, aloe, cedar, honey, pomegranates, lilies, and roses, to name a few. Perfume and fragrance oils bring joy to the heart, says Proverbs 27:9.

I believe our worship has a scent as well. Mary took her most expensive perfume and poured it all over Jesus' feet and wiped it with her hair to anoint Him for burial. I am convinced that scent is a massive part of Heaven's Culture! I believe we will hear more and more of heavenly encounters that involve scent.

In the testimony above, I really love the fact that red wine was the scent that showed up during that supernatural experience. Red wine symbolizes Love, the new covenant, the blood of Jesus, the washing of our sins, freedom, Holy Spirit, and life!

MONEY MIRACLES

So, who doesn't love a good money miracle testimony? I know I do! God is our Provider; the earth is the Lord's and the fullness thereof; He owns the cattle on a thousand hills. He thought it would be a great idea to put a gold coin in a fish's mouth to help pay the temple taxes, as the bible tells us. God owns it all! So why not expect God to show up in fun, miraculous ways when it comes to providing for us too?

A few years back, a friend of mine and I attended another friend's wedding. During that time in my life, I was a stay-at-home mom. As a family, we decided that we wanted to be there full time for our kids, especially during those early years, and so my husband went to work, and I stayed home. This left us with only one income and, after taking care of the bills, it didn't leave much wiggle room for anything else.

While attending this wedding with my friend, she graciously offered to pay for the wedding gift but have both our names put on it. How kind! Grateful as I was for the gesture, I still wanted to try and contribute to the gift financially as best I could.

My friend came to pick me up at my place, so we could drive together. But, before getting into her car, I wanted to check my wallet again. I went to my car and started to dig through it to see if I had anything at all that I could contribute to this wedding gift, something…anything – if I could. I must have dug through every crease and crevice of my wallet three or four times, only to come up empty-handed. I had nothing to give. In an effort to hurry up, I now tossed my wallet into the glove compartment, locked the door, and left. For the first five minutes of the car ride, for some reason, I just kept on repeating,

"I have nothing in my wallet; I have nothing in my wallet." This was a little odd, and I took note of that. I remembered even asking myself, "Why do I keep thinking that?" It was a little strange. Okay, maybe one might think about it once or twice but then would move on. I mean, my friend made it clear that she was okay with paying for the gift. The day progressed, and the wedding was lovely. After it was over, my friend dropped me back off at home.

The next morning, I had to run out, so I got to my car, unlocked the door, and got in. I opened my glove compartment to grab my wallet to put into my purse, and something told me to open it first, and so I did. I unzipped the zipper – and there sticking out like a sore thumb – were three five-dollar bills. I gasped because I knew that I knew I'd searched this wallet repeatedly the day before and found nothing. You wouldn't miss three bills sticking out in the first part of your wallet like that even if you had only looked once! I now knew why I kept repeating those thoughts. God wanted me to remember nothing was in there the last time I checked.

Somehow, the money appeared supernaturally. It's easier to believe that than thinking that someone broke into my car to give me cash and not steal anything. I know God blessed me that day with fifteen dollars. I know He did that specifically because He wanted to highlight these numbers for me too.

Three, five, and fifteen stand for:
3 = Completion
5 = Grace
15 = Rest

I am Complete in Christ because of Grace, and I can Rest in Him and in that reality all the days of my life…always! Nothing lacking; nothing missing! The Sabbath day of rest to me is not just a day in the week – it's a state of being in Christ every day of my life!

God is our Provider. He's never failed us, nor will He ever – you can take that to the bank! Thank you, Jesus, for Your faithfulness.

THE FERRIS WHEEL ANGEL

Shortly after the radical encounter that I shared in chapter one happened, God started to really pull me in. I found myself getting radically changed from the inside out. Depression that I struggled with was replaced with joy; some long-time addictions and bad habits were suddenly giving way to a sense of freedom.

I started to spend five or six hours a day just reading my grandfather's old leather bible that I had found deep in the back of a closet somewhere. Truth be told, I still use that bible to this day, which looks well-thumbed, hoping that it doesn't completely fall apart on me. But I'd rather that than a bible untouched and in perfect condition.

I did this for months and months every single day. As a matter of fact, my stepfather witnessed such a radical change come over me that he himself said he found the Lord. For me to go through the transformation that I did, God must be real, he thought. And, of course, he was right!

This day, I was hours into my reading and praying and spending time with the Lord when it was nearing 3:00 pm. Suddenly, I got exhausted, and I decided to take a nap. I lay down on my bed and looked at the clock on my side table, and it read exactly 3:00 pm. As soon as I saw the time, I was out like a light. Not a minute later, not 30 seconds later, right in that moment, I was utterly and completely pulled into a deep, peaceful sleep.

I felt like I went more into a vision rather than a dream, though; but just like Paul said, "In the body or out of the body I cannot tell, God knows" (2 Corinthians 12:3). In this vision, I found myself on a massive Ferris wheel that was so huge that I was in the Heavens when it got to the very peak of its climb. When it got to the top it stopped and as I looked around, I could not see the ground, I was surrounded by nothing but beautiful fluffy white clouds. Suddenly an angel came down above my head. This angel felt like an old friend, as if we had known each other. It reached out to me. Doing so was hard for him and for me, and as we did, I woke up.

I looked around the room expecting it to be night but was shocked to find out it wasn't –the clock now read 3:05 pm. Only five minutes had passed from when I first lay down and passed out instantly. I had gone to sleep feeling extremely tired, but now only five minutes later, I was up again feeling like I had the best and most restful sleep of my life. I felt I was gone for hours when it was only five minutes in actual time. It was so sweet to see that angel and to have us connect and then to wake in such a renewed and restful state. God sends His angels to help in different ways, but whatever the way, they are ministering to our needs. *"Are not all angels ministering spirits sent to serve those who will inherit salvation?"* says Hebrews 1:14. That angel was sent to strengthen me, and I'm so grateful!

THE VASE

One night, my husband and I were at a leadership church meeting in the home of the pastor's friend. It was a night of close fellowship, and the spirit of prophecy was moving. The fifteen of us were in this spacious cozy sunken den and mostly seated on a large u-shaped couch. In front of us was a coffee table looking on to a nice gas fireplace adorned with personal touches plus home decor pieces. On the floor to the right of the fireplace was this three-foot-tall vase. The pastor was going around to each one of us, giving us individual words and praying for us that night. A little after he was done, we broke out into casual chat among ourselves. At one point, for some reason, my attention was drawn in the direction of the floor vase.

Now, this part gets a little tricky to try and explain because, once again, the experience is totally out of this world, but I will do my best. As I am looking at this vase, I see the face of Jesus pass by in a reflection in the broad section of the vase. I immediately became aware that we as a group were supposed to gather together and have that vase poured out over us. I got everyone's attention and shared what I'd seen and heard from the Lord. I asked if there was anything in the vase, and there was not. It was totally empty, just there for show.

Everyone seemed ready for it, so we all gathered on the wide steps leading up from the den into the dining room and, even still, a few extra spilled onto the dining room level floor, but we managed to all be together. Steve, the owner of the home, volunteered to do the pouring.

We were all anticipating what might happen when God moved, especially on me. I mean, it was completely out there. I see the face of Jesus in the vase, and now we are all standing waiting for this empty fireplace decor piece to be poured over us – the craziest thing to say the least!

So here we go. Steve lifts the vase slightly over his head and starts to tip it over. As soon as he does...the back row of people get HIT with the glory and power of God and fall out – some even get thrown a few feet back. As the tipping continues over us, the next row gets HIT, and they too fall out under the power of God, and finally, while the vase is completely tipped over, the last and third row gets HIT too.

The Glory of God just broke out on all of us: many of us got soaked up in the joy of the Lord with laughter. Others were shaking and manifesting, and some just enjoyed the chill. If we don't know by now, God can't be put in a box; however, in this case, He made like a genie and filled the vase. It was mind-blowing coupled with experiencing the real tangible love from God. He showed up that night to pour out over us, and He did it in a way none of us ever could ever have imagined.

Every day is a new day to expect and believe for God to pour out His love over you. Look for Him to do so today and this week. He gets excited when you expect Him to do so, and He's not one to disappoint.

I'M GOING TO SPEAK TO YOU TONIGHT

One morning when I woke up, I heard God speak these words to me very clearly,

"I'm going to speak to you tonight."

I was attending a three-day annual church conference that weekend, and it was now day two. I kept the information quietly to myself and was so excited I just couldn't wait to hear what God wanted to say to me through one of His prophets that night.

My friend and I arrived at church that night to try and find a good spot – for me, secretly close to the front so the guest speaker could find me. There were at least 2000 people present, so I wanted to do my part to help God by trying to be visible and easily found. Right? So, we managed to snag some seats that were a little off to the side of the center stage but still in the front row. Just then, one of our friends in security asked my friend and me if we could move all the way to the back row to help with security and people's needs. Of course, we were happy to help, but deep down, I was crushed – I had been so excited about getting my word all day, and now I thought there was no way. So, I said to the Father, "But now, how are You going to find me all the way back there?"

I heard the Holy Spirit laugh gently and say, "I'm God, I can find you anywhere."

Wow, it's amazing how only one word from God can change everything! Immediately my spirit was lifted as we moved all the way to the back.

"Yeah, you are totally right, God; you can find me anywhere," I chuckled back at Him, "I should have known!"

The night was amazing, and the speaker was ending with his message. I was still waiting patiently to hear the word God wanted to share with me. The guest finished his messages, came to a complete close and was heading to leave the stage.

As he was walking off the long stage and almost out of sight completely, I said to the Lord, "Well, I guess I'll be getting my word tomorrow." But the certainty of it was settled within me then and there. I knew that I knew God was going to give me a word through that man of God.

Just then, the speaker stopped, turned around, walked back to the podium, took the mic, looked directly into my direction at the back of the church, among 2000 people, then pointed and said, "I have a word from God for you!"

I just smiled widely and said, "Okay, God, here we go!" while the people around me were asking with hand gestures if it was for them. We were so packed together that, had I not already known the word was for me, I would have done the same. The speaker said no to everyone, called me out, and asked me to step into the aisle. I did as he asked and, as he started to prophesy the word that God had for me, I felt like a flame of fire. My entire body was burning with such heat, not painful but just W.O.W intense. It became an all-consuming fire. I could sense a very large angel behind me as well. It was totally amazing!

I share this testimony with you to point out how much God is on it. The Holy Spirit can find you anywhere. Even right now, He's mindful of you, and His love can reach you! Respond by reaching back, knowing He hears you.

YOUR SHADOW WILL HEAL THEM

Another night my husband and I were out with some people we had recently met. We were having an enjoyable time with lots of good conversation. But at some point, in the night, the conversation took a bit of a turn for me. One of the new people that we had met had said they "sensed" something about me – and not in a good way either. I knew this was not true, but just the thought of it totally broke me. I don't think it showed on my face, but deep down, I was suddenly a total mess. The defeated enemy had a plan to accuse me and bring me down that night. To be honest, I can't even remember the exact words he used, but I just remember how downcast I became. Just the thought of me not pleasing God or Him being disappointed in me was more than I could bear.

The next night we had a special conference at church, and I still couldn't shake off the feeling. I had spent most of the day, and now the night, beating myself up, but I couldn't seem to shake out of this funk I was in. The church was packed. Almost all the 500 seats were full, and people were lined up at the back and against the walls too. The worship was amazing as usual; everyone was giving their all to God, but for the life of me, all I could do was sit there and tell Him, "God, I'm sorry for disappointing You so badly." The tears were uncontrollable. I don't remember ever feeling so bad about myself. No matter what I did or said to God helped me to move past this extreme sorrow.

After about an hour or so, the Pastor got up on the stage and had a word of knowledge for healing. He called those with ankle injuries up to the front. Four people came up the front and stood in a row close to the stage. It was already packed, so people had to back up a bit to make some room. Just then, I decided to take a pause from all my misery and look up to see what was happening. Being a part of the ministry team, we were seated close to the front to be ready to help minister to those in need. I had zero intention of going up at all that night to pray for anyone. I could barely stand up out of my seat myself because of my heaviness; much else, pray for someone else. As I tuned in for a second and looked at the four people now standing at the front in need of healing, I heard the Lord say clearly, "Walk past them, and your shadow will heal them!"

In bewilderment, I managed to squeeze out a weak, "Uh?" First, I thought to myself, "Is God even paying attention? If He was, He would know that I totally suck! I mean, I'd just spent the last hour telling Him all about it. Did He happen to miss it? And my shadow will be used to heal people? Isn't that like level 10 of supernatural healing? I'm not even sure I qualify to be used at level 1 right now. I don't always feel qualified on a good day, never mind today! Anyone else?"

Just then, the pastor calls me up to the front to pray for them. "Oh God, now you're just being funny!" I thought. There were at least 25 other people on the ministry team that he could have easily called and were closer too. Still in my seat, drying my eyes, I did what I was asked and walked to the front to pray for these four. On my way up, I started to take God's comment about my shadow healing the sick a little more seriously.

You know how Peter's shadow did the same thing in Acts 5:15. The sick were laid out on the street, so they could be touched by Peter's shadow when he walked by. Now, I have seen miracles before, and I have prayed for people who have gotten healed, but the whole shadow thing wasn't even on my grid. Here you have super anointed Peter in the bible healing people with his shadow, but who was I to do the same? That thought had never even crossed my mind up until that point.

As I made my way to the front, I didn't have a plan or even a fancy prayer to pray. I was just going to stretch out my hands and pass by them like God said to do. There were large stage lights behind the pulpit pointing at the stage to highlight the preacher on the stage, but also by default it provided a shadow for anyone at the altar as well.

Coming to the first person, I stretched out my hand and barely touched them as I walked by, they instantly fell out under the power of God. Same with the second and the third person too. When the first three all got back up to standing position again, all four were asked to test out their former injuries by doing something they could not do before. The four of them started to run around the church and by the time they made their way back to the altar they professed that they were completely healed.

Praise God for the miraculous! God said, greater works shall we do in John 14:12. I don't know about you but I'm ready to see, believe and walk completely, in those greater works every day! Matthew 10 vs 8 puts it plain as well. It reads that we are too, heal the sick, cleanse the lepers, raise the dead, and cast out devils: for freely have we received, freely we are to give.

I share this radical encounter with you because I want you to know that God doesn't see us the same way regardless of how we sometimes see ourselves. God didn't even bat an eye at all the internal accusations we keep bashing ourselves with, accusations that defeated Satan uses to tear us down. He didn't even address them. As far as God was concerned, I was a new creature in Christ Jesus, and He focused on that. He wants you to do that same thing. After I went back to my seat, I was instantly delivered of shame and condemnation. Thank You, God!

Chapter 8

The Prophetic

I know what the prophetic has done for me in my life and in many other people's lives as well. If you aren't sure what the prophetic is or how it's able to bless you and others, then my hope and prayer for you is that, after reading this chapter, you get to see, understand, and move more in the prophetic. There are a ton of books out there already that go deep into this gift. That's not my goal here. My goal here is to just give you some of the basics and lay a foundation for the prophetic.

But first, let me give you an illustration of how the prophetic has played a part in my life. Take this book, for example. There have been many moving parts and facets that have helped make this book into a reality, and I can boldly say without a shadow of a doubt, prophecy played a big part in that!

Over the years, God had used people to speak prophetically into my life about this book and other books that would come after this. Some of the people He used I knew and some I had never met before.

The first time I ever got a word about writing books was over fifteen years ago. It came at a time where I think deep down inside, I had a teeny tiny desire to share what God has done for me in the form of a book. I was just so grateful and in awe of what He did in the testimony that you read in chapter one and in other areas of my life, that I didn't feel like it was meant to be kept all to myself, but rather sharing it to bless others too. I knew He would get more glory by sharing it than not. But the thought was also quickly snuffed out due to a lot of self-doubt at the time about ever being able to write a book. It wasn't something that I'd ever really thought I would be capable of doing.

To give you some background, growing up, I had the hardest time reading and writing to the point where I was evaluated by a specialist at about the age of seven and diagnosed with a severe learning disability. At the time, it had been almost three years since I had been secretly being abused by a family member. My immediate family knew nothing about it, and I think, looking back, that incident may have played a big role in affecting my ability to learn in school.

God has brought me a long way since and has healed me of all things that could come out of those situations, including the area of learning.

I remember getting my first breakthrough when I was eleven. I recall trying to read during independent reading time, a class I always dreaded. However, on this day, while I was on the second page of the first chapter of a new book, suddenly everything just clicked into place, and I could read with ease what was on the page. I was so blown away because moments before, I struggled as usual just to read a sentence.

However, even after that encounter, it was still a process for me to learn and grow in reading and spelling and even more in my self-esteem. Despite getting better and better every year, the label of being dumb and unable to read or write stuck with me. I have had to overcome a lot of embarrassment and personal humiliation growing up as these thoughts pursued me, even into adulthood.

I remember being in my early thirties, married, and a mom of two at the time, when I mentioned writing a book, and this person had remarked, "Don't you think you should know how to spell first if you are going to write a book?" We were only Facebook friends, and I guess he saw some of my posts that had spelling mistakes. You see, it wasn't that I could not spell more than it was that often my thoughts would jump so far ahead of my words that I still didn't always catch the mistakes. It seemed to be a skill that wasn't my strong suit. Thankfully, even as I write this book, things have improved greatly from where I started, and I'm happy to report I've also ditched the shame and embarrassment I used to have around this struggle of mine.

Paul was a big advocate of overcoming shame and embarrassment about our weaknesses. When he groans about his weaknesses, God says to him, "*My grace is sufficient for you, for my power is made perfect in weakness*" (2 Corinthians 12:9). Therefore, he says he will boast all the more gladly about his weaknesses so that Christ's power may rest on him.

Fast Forward now to the beginning of 2020, and this "desire" to write this book called *Radical Encounters with God* once again started to stir in me. Sometime around the end of spring 2020, I started the first step of getting the initial outline for the book done, which I ended up doing. But then I paused after that. I wanted to make sure that God wanted me to do this. I wanted His green light, and I wouldn't move forward without it.

Around the same time, all sorts of conflicting thoughts started to come my way, as I think they often do when we consider stepping out of the boat. "What would people think?" "What if people didn't believe that these radical encounters were true?" "What if they didn't believe in God?" "What if some of these testimonies were just too radical for the body of Christ?" "What if someone didn't like my book?" "What if, what if, what if…"

But in the end, it boiled down to this conversation: "God, even with my present insecurities and my 'what if's,' I want to know what You want more. If You want me to share these personal stories and testimonies with others and put them out there for Your name's sake, then I'm willing." It was a "here I am Lord, use me" moment.

I realized that all my what ifs combined were not worthy of being compared to the glory that I believe Jesus would have from me sharing my experiences and testimonies with whomever it was meant to be shared with. God is for testimony sharing. He gets great joy out of that. It is so much more than just sharing a feel-good story or just tickling your ears.

The bible says that we overcome by the blood of the lamb and the word of our testimonies and did not love our lives (our pride) to the death (Revelation 12:11). We also know that the testimony of Jesus is the spirit of prophecy (Revelation 19:10). Testimonies have the ability to bring light into dark places and share hope with the hopeless. Testimonies also have a way of disarming fear, worry, and doubt in others. But mostly, they bring a glory explosion offering to God.

And so, during this summer of 2020, I was seeking confirmation once and for all, for this desire that I had popped up for the last two decades or to whether I should write this book and secondly, if so, is now the time? I was willing to write this book, but being willing wasn't enough for me; I was looking to Heaven for its thumbs up and all systems a-go confirmation! Many people are not comfortable with hand clapping in a church service or speaking in tongues or praying for the sick and believing in healing on a Sunday because it distracts from the program. So, this book is probably going to get some seriously religious folks' panties in a wad at the very least. Which is fine because that's what a religious spirit does best, tries to control and gets offended at all things Jesus related. But still as I was willing to write, I just wasn't willing without Heaven's green light. I didn't write this book for my own sake and if God is for you, who can be against you? So, to pause and wait for an answer, seemed like the right next step to take. Without telling anyone, secretly in my heart, I began asking for confirmation and waiting to hear back.

It was also about that time that I started watching live broadcasts online as many events and gatherings were being shut down and online was the place to go to connect.

One Friday night in mid-August, as I was watching a live online broadcast, I was highlighted for a word. The person began with:

"Melissa, I just see the fire of God all over you! I see you as a burning one, and I see the Lord has given you stories and testimonies that you need to tell!"

My heart started pounding with excitement and awe as one's heart often would when they feel God and the tears started to flow down my face. It has, after all, been twenty years in the making.

That was it: this was the confirmation that I needed to hear after asking and waiting for the last few weeks.

Even though I had only just started the outline and hadn't "officially" worked on chapters yet, it immediately became settled in my spirit that this was a Go! I had written in the comments section of Facebook live that I was writing a book full of my personal testimonies to let him know. The person continued to speak and share what the Lord was saying: how our father is proud that I am listening and being obedient with moving forward in writing this book and how these encounters shared will touch a multitude of lives.

You can see from this story how prophecy had a direct and powerful impact on my life, and, because of this, prophecy will directly impact other people's lives as well. That's the beautiful thing about it.

I often get asked this question, "How do I hear the voice of God and prophecy myself?"

Well, first off, let's look at this scripture:

But when you pray, you must believe and not doubt at all. Whoever doubts is like a wave in the sea that is driven and blown about by the wind. If you are like that, unable to make up your mind and undecided in all you do, you must not think that you will receive anything from the Lord (James 1:6-8).

A lot of people want to hear the voice of God, but at the same time, they aren't even sure that God even speaks to them.

To that, I would say: Many Christians don't have a hearing problem: they have a believing problem.

The bible says, "My sheep know my voice…and a stranger they will not follow." So, ask yourself, "Am I, His sheep?" Are you saved by faith through grace?

If the answer to those questions is yes, then you need to agree with the bible promise on this one and start believing that you can hear His voice. If you need help believing, there's an assurance for that too. The bible says, *"So then faith comes by hearing and hearing by the word of God"* (Romans 10:17 NKJV). Get your face in the word of God more, and believing will be just one of the many amazing treasures that come out of that act. When you have that argument settled within you once and for all, you can move on with confidence.

Now that you know you hear His voice because you are His sheep, and the bible says you do, it's a matter of listening and learning.

Samuel was a mighty prophet of God. But still, even though Samuel was dedicated to the Lord as a child, he, too, had to learn to recognize the voice of God. One night he was asleep just outside the tabernacle when he heard his name being called.

Then God called out, "Samuel, Samuel! "Samuel answered, "Yes? I'm here." Then he ran to Eli saying, "I heard you call. Here I am." Eli said, "I didn't call you. Go back to bed." And so, he did. God called again, "Samuel, Samuel!" Samuel got up and went to Eli, "I heard you call. Here I am." Again, Eli said, "Son, I didn't call you. Go back to bed." (This all happened before Samuel knew God for himself. It was before the revelation of God had been given to him personally.) God called again, "Samuel!"—the third time! Yet again Samuel got up and went to Eli, "Yes? I heard you call me. Here I am" That's when it dawned on Eli that God was calling the boy. So, Eli directed Samuel, "Go back and lie down. If the voice calls again, say, 'Speak, God. I'm your servant, ready to listen.'" Samuel returned to his bed. Then God came and stood before him exactly as before, calling out, "Samuel! Samuel!" Samuel answered, "Speak. I'm your servant, ready to listen" (1 Samuel 3:4-10).

Another key takeaway here is that Samuel had a mentor, Eli, the priest, to guide him. You may have someone like that in your life that can teach and help you learn and grow; if not, there are many resources out there that you can pull from, books, commentaries, online courses, churches, and many more.

In this incident, Samuel was hearing the audible voice of God. Not everyone will hear God like that; nevertheless, God has put spiritual receptors in all of us to be able to receive and respond to Him. It's like the wind. When the wind blows, you don't see it; but look at how the ocean responds to it with giant waves, trees respond by their branches swaying, or the wind roars. In the same way, we have the ability to respond when God speaks to us.

Our physical bodies are loaded with receptors. These receptors have the unique ability to sense the slightest of changes like light, heat, or other external stimuli. Once picked up, they send a signal to the sensory nerves, and our sensory nerves carry these signals to the spinal cord and brain, where they are processed.

When God speaks, it can be in the form of a feeling, a knowing, an impression, an audible voice, or a thought. It can also come as a picture, still or in motion. And, although these things might seem hard to pick up because you have feelings, emotions, and thoughts constantly going on within yourself, you will get more and more familiar with hearing and knowing the voice of God over time. So always seek, listen to, and even practice sharing what you have heard with others so it can be tested and weighed.

In whatever way it comes across to you, when God speaks to you, you will start to sense an "added" element that accompanies the feeling, the thought, the knowing, the impression, and sometimes the audible voice. The addition can simply be a gut feeling deep down in you, but it will be something that is different from your day-to-day, minute-to-minute norm. It simply has a greater weight to it. Even if it's a still small voice – and oftentimes it is – it still has a stand-out quality to it because it is God.

If our bodies are able to sense and pick up the slightest change in light or heat, how much more our spirits?

Growing in the prophetic also requires that you take risks. The main risk is in opening your mouth and possibly getting it wrong. Even as I write this book, I have prophesied many times. Many times, God will give me specifics, but not all of them have 100% landed. I could have stopped and given up right there and then, but I have a heart to see people touched and miraculously experience God through the prophetic. And so, I just keep going and leaning into it.

Just last night, I spoke to someone and quietly asked God in my heart to give me something for this lady that would touch and bless her. I felt like she could use that. I did not know her personally, nor are we currently friends on Facebook or any other social media where I could read about her background. So, I didn't know anything personal about her.

As I pressed in, God gave me specific words of knowledge about those she loved but moved on to Heaven, including the exact date one of them passed. Also, He shared with me things that she had just finished saying to someone the day before, which were a confirmation to her. Obviously, I was not with her that day, and as a matter of fact, we don't even live in the same country, but God was with her as He is with all of us and knows all things. And, lastly, He gave me names as well. God showed me a pair of Levi jeans, and I asked if she knew anyone with the name Levi. As it turned out, that was a family member of hers, one she hadn't been in touch within a little while, who I believe God wanted her to connect with and check in on them. She said that this encounter was much needed and blessed her greatly.

Another recent time, I was at a gas station paying the cashier when I saw in the spirit the name Jenny printed on a sash, which was encircled around her and moving clockwise slowly. I asked her if she knew and had anyone by the name of Jenny in her close circle. As it turned out, Jenny was her best friend, and from there, God gave me a much-needed timely word for Jenny to be passed to her by her best friend, the cashier.

All of this took a risk on my part. I could not have said anything out of fear of missing the mark or looking dumb, but I'm willing to step out, if it means God will get the glory and lives will be touched by His love. This is just one of many stories where God has used me to prophesy and lean on Him each time. Without Him, I couldn't do a thing. If you want to grow in the prophetic, you need to be prepared to step out and take risks.

How is prophecy different from a word of knowledge? Word of knowledge falls under the prophetic umbrella and is in the same gifting category. It can be used often with prophecy, but it has some of its own characteristics. Prophecy, among many things, is used by God to share future events, whether that is one minute from now or a hundred years from now. Words of knowledge oftentimes, but not limited to, share about things that have already happened, things that are happening now or are about to happen.

Once, for example, I had a mental picture of a series of numbers along with a location, and I did not know what they meant. It turns out that those numbers were the coordinates for a military tour of duty for a person who was in this meeting with us, and the location was where some of those in the tour where born. Again, I did not know this person personally; neither had I met him before: but God knew him and wanted to speak to him. He was having a hard time accepting God's love because he didn't feel worthy of it but, sharing these details with him was a way to encourage him to open up to God and receive His unconditional love.

Another time as I was prophesying over this lady, God took the prophetic direction towards her two-year-old granddaughter. During the middle of the prophetic conversation, I saw a beautiful red ruby gemstone. I didn't know if this was connected to her or if it was for someone else there. One thing I've learned is to keep going and digging in for more details. When one or two of them don't land with the person you are speaking to, then it's time to move on and see who those details could be for. So, I asked the lady if a red ruby meant anything to her, and she gasped. I thought maybe it was the stone of her birth month or something, but her reaction indicated something more. It turns out Ruby was the name of her granddaughter's dog, and so the details God was giving me were still for her and her granddaughter, so I kept going.

As you can see, Words of knowledge tend to be either on point or not because they can get very detailed and hit the mark.

At times you may get a word of knowledge before the prophetic word comes. Sometimes it's God's way of pointing the right person that matches those details out to you correctly so you can then move on to prophesying over them. Other times, it's so that the person, who may not otherwise believe in God or the gifts of the Spirit, can see His power and love in action. It's hard to deny something when you see it with your own eyes, or it happens to you. Other times still, it may just be for someone else who is witnessing it all happen. When you don't know someone, and you start to "read their mail," and they know there's no way you could ever have known that and you point to God being the source, it changes their lives.

God wants to talk to you. He's enraptured by you, and He wants to share His thoughts and plans with you. Amos 3:7 says, *"Surely the Sovereign LORD does nothing without revealing his plan to his servants the prophets."* He showed His plan to Moses when it was time to deliver His people out of bondage. He did that with Abraham when He planned to destroy Sodom and Gomorrah. He did it with Elijah when He was going to call down rain for the first time in three years. There are countless prophecies in the Old Testament concerning the crucifixion, especially in Isaiah 53, which is central to the entire conversation between God and His prophets. Although there are many, here are a few more examples of how in the end, these prophetic pictures all point to the main event of History: Jesus dying on the cross and His love for us. I mentioned this in a previous chapter, but I wanted to elaborate a bit more here. When you start to read the Old Testament after this on your own, you will start to pick up parts of it yourself that stand out as being prophetic pictures that point the way to Jesus.

In Exodus 16, God fed the Israelites in the wilderness every morning with manna, the bread from Heaven. That was a prophetic picture of Jesus Christ, the Bread of Life Himself, who came down from Heaven. Now that we have the real manna, Jesus, we are to feed on Him daily to have the understanding and strength to face each new day.

Many of the characters in the bible represent Jesus in so many ways. Job, the man who was loyal to God despite overwhelming trials, is a picture of Jesus the innocent Lamb who went to the slaughter without saying a word. Satan was betting with God that if he pushed Job just hard enough, Job would curse God and die, the same way he tested Jesus in the wilderness. Job losing his family in one blow was a picture of the family of God being lost all in a moment in the garden. Job's physical trials and humiliation represented Jesus during His trial and crucifixion, but in the end, Job received a double reward after he forgave and prayed for his friends. In the end, all was restored and more, the same way that Jesus rose on the third day and received the highest honor in Heaven!

Daniel in the lion's den represents Jesus in Hell. Both had been convicted and punished unjustly. But just like angels were sent to shut the lions' months in the pit, leaving Daniel untouched, so did Jesus remain untouched during those days and nights in hell after His death Not only did, He remain untouched, but He was about to deal a defeating blow to the enemy. Both Daniel and Jesus rose out of their pits supernaturally. Furthermore, with Daniel, the king ordered that those men who schemed and plotted Daniel's downfall were to be thrown into the den themselves along with family members so that their entire lineage would be erased. In the same way, *"having disarmed the powers and authorities, Jesus made a public spectacle of them, (Satan and his demons), triumphing over them by the cross"* (Colossians 2:15, emphasis added).

JESUS AND THE TEMPLE

Jesus entered the temple court and drove out all who were buying and selling there. He overturned the tables of the moneychangers and the benches of those selling doves. *"It is written,"* He said to them, *"'My house will be called a house of prayer,' but you are making it 'a den of robbers'"* (Matthew 21:12-13). Jesus also declared, *"Destroy this temple, and I will raise it again in three days"* (John 2:19). Biblically speaking, this represents you and me as being the temple of God and Jesus overturning and driving out everything that doesn't belong. He accomplished all this in the days during His death and resurrection.

God can also speak prophetically using dreams and visions. As I mentioned in previous chapters, these spiritual gifting's often go hand in hand and can overlap because the same Holy Spirit gives them to whomever He chooses (1 Corinthians 12:1-11). So don't get used to just one way of expecting God to speak to you. And when you do get a word from God, whether that is through a dream, a vision, an audible voice, or perhaps a feeling or knowing, and it's for someone else, it's good to check in with God about other details too. "What do You want me to do with this? Do you want me to share this with them? Do you want me to share it now, or is there a better time? Is this something You want me to just pray into? "

Often, I notice God will have me share it with the other person relatively soon – not always – but for the most part. The whole point of prophecy is to strengthen others, encourage them, and comfort them, and there's no time like the present (1 Corinthians 14:3). Of course, it's always good to check in with God first.

Another characteristic of the prophetic is, oftentimes, God will confirm it more than once, especially if it points to a future event. With a word of knowledge and, more specifically, one that is pointing to the past, you don't need two or three words of knowledge to tell the person their birthday or home address or the name of their pet like Ruby the dog, in the story I already shared. One is all you need, and it either is or isn't. When it comes to future things, because none of us are in it yet, when two or three people start hearing and saying the exact same thing as God, it has more credibility, plus God gets all the glory as He reveals future things to come with 2 or 3 or more once they come to pass as He always should. And when it concerns you personally, that confirmation also includes Him telling you the same thing Himself. I can't tell you how many times I have prophesied to someone, and they say, "Omigosh, I just thought that today," or "I just had that conversation with God last night!" Make no mistake: Jesus is the real MVP of prophecy, and He can speak to you better than anyone.

Something to keep in mind as you are growing in the gift of prophecy is that you should not project your own unsettled issues. At times I have seen people try to prophesy, but it didn't come out of a place of intimacy with God. It came out of their own personal troubles and, at times, their own warped views of the Father and the Gospel. On the flip side, be careful, too, of what you receive as a prophetic word for yourself. Not everyone who says they are, really are! Wolves in sheep's clothing is a real thing.

Again, if you are new to the prophetic and are learning and growing in hearing the voice of God, and you get it wrong, I believe there is grace for that. Hey, I'm just glad that you showed up and tried. That doesn't mean you won't get it bang on the first time; I've seen that happen, but just in case, keep it up and keep going; before long, you will be confident in hearing the voice of God! Sometimes a pastor's first sermon is not as good as his hundred and twenty-second sermon, right? It's ok to let people know that you are practicing and growing in this area as well. At the end of the day, we are learning and growing no matter who you are that will never stop.

Also, it's important to point out that the Father is love, and therefore a word, even if it is corrective in nature, will have love covering it. Even when they are being corrected by their father, my kids know that they are still loved and tend to draw closer to him afterwards because godly correction means you care. That's what happened when the Lord chastened the people of Nineveh through the prophet Jonah. It changed the direction of the entire nation and drew them back to God (Jonah 3:1-10).

What's exciting about the prophetic gift, too, is it's transferable. This is why it's important to surround yourself with those who are walking in it already (even remotely) if you want to grow your prophetic gifting. Or get your hands on some good resources. King Saul was not a prophet, but the prophetic anointing fell upon him when he associated with prophetic people: "*When he and his servant arrived at Gibeah, a procession of prophets met him; the Spirit of God came powerfully upon him, and he joined in their prophesying*" (1 Samuel 10:10).

Chapter 9

Radical Encounters and Testimonies Part IV

THEY'RE GONE!

Sometimes deliverance just looks like having the right understanding of what Jesus has done for us on the cross. Once you do that, you will notice a significant change. You will find joy where depression used to be; you will find peace instead of worry. You will just simply be happy! Where you once felt empty and restless and couldn't exactly put your finger on it, you now are feeling satisfied and calm. For those who have been there, you know that's a miracle in and of itself.

And there are other times when deliverance comes in the form of casting out demons. Sometimes that can look "messy," and other times, that can look like one quick swing of the sword that cuts through and divides. Either way, God loves people and wants to see all set free.

One day during a prayer meeting, I noticed this girl who was kneeling and praying quietly off in a corner by herself. God kept directing my attention to her. She wasn't doing anything out of the ordinary that would make me say she was wrestling with a defeated demon or anything like that; I just felt like something was "off." This is known as discernment. I felt like the Lord wanted me to go over and pray for her. So, I went over and asked if I could pray for her, and she said yes.

Getting close to her, I could see that she seemed desperate to be set free. There indeed was a demon tormenting her on the inside, which I could sense. I prayed for her and her deliverance for a few minutes doing what the bible says in Mark 16:17-18: *"...these signs will accompany those who believe. In my name they will drive out demons; they will speak in new tongues, they will lay their hands on the sick, and they will be made well"* (BSB). I commanded those defeated demons to go and leave her alone.

When we finished, I could see her whole countenance shift. She lifted her head, looked around, then looked and me, took a big breath, and with a sigh of relief said, "They're gone; they are really, really gone!"

There was no big scene or show; in this case, it was just a quiet and discreet matter-of-fact kind of deliverance. I wasn't there to negotiate. Her temple, which houses the Holy Spirit, already had an owner. It was already paid for by the Blood of the Lamb, who was slain before the foundation of the world. There was no need to talk about it. They had to go! And I think the girl I was praying for really appreciated it being that way too, private and away from a crowd. God is not in the business of embarrassing His children as sometimes people feel in a situation like that. In all truth, all of us go through some form of deliverance at some time in our lives, and it's nothing to feel ashamed about either; rather, it's something to be celebrated. Thank God for deliverance. Being set free is a radical encounter indeed!

BAG OF SHROOMS

Well, if you are wondering if this one has to do with the drug Mushrooms, then, yes you would be correct. This encounter happened during a time in my life that was dark. At that time, just about everything I was doing seemed to be counterproductive and self-sabotaging. I was very depressed and sad, and most of the time just wanted to feel numb and not feel any more pain.

This night I was hanging around this girl who had asked me if I could drive her to the church youth group night. She said it was a part of her probation outline rules. Now I've heard of community service, but I've never heard of having to go to a youth service at church as part of someone's probation period. Nevertheless, I went with the flow and took her there. It was a cold Wednesday night, and I had no other plans.

Before we got there, she pulled out a bag of mushrooms, and well, it seemed like a good idea at the time. So, we started eating them. I was a bit surprised because some time had passed, and I didn't feel anything like I normally would. So, I did what seemed the "logical" thing: I ate some more, waited, still nothing, and then ate some more, and more, and then a little bit more. I don't know how much I ate exactly that night, but it was a whole heck of a lot. I just couldn't understand why they weren't kicking in for me yet. My friend was totally feeling it long before I was, and I was feeling left out of the "party."

At the church, we were directed downstairs to what seemed to be a concert. It was a long rectangle room with a stage at the end of it where the band played and sang what I guess was Christian rock music. Up until that point, the only Christian music I'd ever heard was from hymn books! The room was dimly lit with spotlights and rows of chairs. We took a seat, and not too long after, guess what! The shrooms started kicking in once you do –fast and furious. I guess eating all those shrooms was just a delayed reaction. But because of how much I had eaten, when it hit, it hit big time, much to my distress.

Imagine tripping out in this church basement of all places! I was very much used to being high, but this was different, and I think I started to panic a little. So, I decided to cry out to God in that moment: "God, please take this away. I know I'm sitting here in church high as a kite, but I don't feel so good, and I'm asking that You please just make it go away."

Well, to my shock and surprise, I felt like a wave passing over me and, as it did, it took my high with it. Within a matter of seconds, I went from being completely wrecked on mushrooms to 100% sober. Within seconds, I was totally back in my right state of mind. I just sat there in disbelief and thankfulness. I didn't feel like I had prayed some special prayer. I mean, if I were to really think about it, I wasn't really all that convinced that Jesus was even hearing me or paying attention to anything I had to say. Who am I that He is mindful of me? I had no idea that I was seen by Him, let alone rescued from myself and my bad choices. In my humiliation, I didn't even tell my friend what happened. I was so beside myself that God had heard me and touched me in that moment; it just felt too intimate to share. But in my heart, I was so thankful that He did. God is so merciful and loving, and He's with us even in our darkest times.

God continued to pour out His love on me, and the desire to use drugs just became less of an issue – and then suddenly, it was gone. There was a time in my life where I thought I would never be free from drugs. I had pictured myself sadly needing them for the rest of my life. But through repentance, God's love and mercy healed and filled me; it replaced all desire for drugs with a desire for His presence. I learned that the best high of all comes from the Highest!

DÉJÀ VU MEETS WORD OF KNOWLEDGE ON STEROIDS

First, a quick explanation about *déjà vu*. *Déjà vu*, simply put, is a French term that means "already seen." *Déjà vu* is an overwhelming sensation you randomly get without warning for a fleeting moment in time that usually lasts a few seconds or so, maybe not even that. It's the feeling like you have been or have lived that moment already. Everything in that moment is exactly how it was the first time you "saw it:" the time of day, clothes you were wearing, words that may have been spoken, people there, or even something as simple as a commercial playing on the TV. It feels a bit like a frozen visual frame or a pause. You just know that moment has happened, and you have been there before, oftentimes feeling like it was in a dream. But how could that be, right?

God knows the first from the last and is not subject to time, including our past, present, or future. He can go in and out of our days as He pleases.

You can revisit the chapters on dreams, visions, and prophecy to learn more about words of knowledge. I believe personally it's a sign and a wonder and can also be a way of God saying to you that your steps are in order, and He's letting you know you are where you are supposed to be. It's like a symbol on a map: you know when you pass the three rocks on the left after the winding river, you're heading in the right direction. I also think that sometimes it can happen more in harder seasons of our life, too, as a way of God saying He's with you through it all. However, if you are a person who does not have déjà vu, not to worry, it doesn't mean you're not where you are supposed to be. So please don't think that!

Also, I coin the title of this story this way because it's not exactly your average *déjà vu* experience. I for sure lived a future moment in my dreams out in time, but it wasn't a short-lived glimpse; instead, it was a very long detailed encounter with a lot of "knowing" elements to it, which gives it that word of knowledge edge.

One late afternoon at home, I must have ended up nodding off to sleep. During that nap, I had a dream about a friend of mine who was at my door. I opened the door, and she was holding an envelope in her hand, which contained money. She had stopped by because she said she and her husband wanted to sow a seed into what I was doing.

Suddenly I woke up. My phone was ringing beside me. On the display, it showed the name of the same friend I was just dreaming about. I did a small eyebrow raise, thinking, "That's funny," as I answered the phone.

"Hey!"

"Hey, I'm outside at your door!"

"You are? That's a little weird. I was just sleeping when you called, and I dreamt you were at my door."

"Really, you did?"

"Yeah, you were holding an envelope! You had money in it that you wanted to give me.

Silence for a moment, and then she asked, "How did you know that?"

"It was all in the dream."

I think we were both blown away by the dream. I mean, it's not the strangest supernatural thing that has ever happened before. But I share this testimony with you because I want to show you that sometimes you are going to just break into the supernatural for no real "apparent" reason because that's just who you are, especially if you walk in the prophetic. But here, in this case, how wonderful that my friend got to know that her giving didn't go unnoticed by God.

How many of you have even wondered that, especially if it was a sacrificial amount in the first place? How amazing it was for her to know that God sees her and is with her. That alone makes that encounter an amazing testimony of God's goodness and love! And God is so faithful. She and her husband are now thriving in their Canadian birthed yet internationally recognized business, doing big things!

JONATHAN'S HOME!

Most of these radical encounters are completely unexpected and totally wild to some degree. This one is no exception.

It was mid-August on a Tuesday night, and usually I would be at church at one of my favorite events of the week, our young adults' night. Hundreds would gather from different churches all over the city to hang out and enjoy the presence of the Lord together. It was always an amazing time.

This night, however, I was at home with my kids in the living room folding clothes when I heard the Lord say, "Jonathan will be there tonight." Now Jonathan was a friend of ours, a much-loved person by all. He served on the ministry team as well. However, he was gone for the whole summer, or so I thought until God said he was going to be at the young adults' night from a mission trip to the other side of the world in Mozambique, Africa.

"Really?" I replied as I grabbed my laptop to watch the live stream, excited to catch a glimpse of him, even if only on screen. I remember just thinking about him, too, the day before, wondering how he was doing and eager to hear all about his trip. With him being there tonight, as the Lord had said it, I was sure he would be sharing with everyone about his mission trip. As I was logging in to my computer, I said to the Lord, "But I thought he wasn't coming back for another few weeks. I guess he's home early."

I got my laptop connected to the live stream and was able to watch from my living room. I was looking around, trying to spot Jonathan, but the camera was pointing at the pastor up on stage as the meeting was almost set to start. Then suddenly, the pastor looked a little shocked, like something had just happened. Moments later, he said, "The craziest thing just happened; Jonathan just appeared to me and spoke these words. He repeated them a few times and then just disappeared."

Silence filled the room for a few seconds while everyone was trying to process what they just heard: basically, our friend appeared to our pastor in a vision-type experience, gave him a message, and then vanished.

Shocked and stunned, with so many thoughts running through my head, I didn't move or speak for a few minutes myself.

"How is that possible, God? You said he would be there, and he was, but then he wasn't! Did he just travel in the spirit?"

"Wait…really? How cool! You're funny, God; You could have added that tiny little detail a few minutes ago, you know? Wow! That's crazy!"

Here I was, at home, minding my kids and folding clothes, when God gave me a heads up, and then Jonathan appeared to our Pastor totally out of the blue to give him a message from the Lord.

You may have heard it before described as Spirit travel or something similar such as teleportation or even transportation. They are a little different from one another in the details but are similar in the sense of their supernatural components. I won't get into all of that here, but you can do some research about this phenomenon if you wish. I will add some incredible biblical stories below and say that it's not something that everybody reads or hears every day, but I do believe God will use these amazing supernatural tools available to the bride of Christ more and more. Perhaps even more so in the days to come, where He will cause his people to supernaturally travel in one form or another to accomplish the things on His heart faster than ever.

I mean, how much time and money would one save if God used them to preach the gospel, heal the sick, raise the dead and speak life to the broken-hearted if they were transported in the Spirit? This is how angels get around most often, unless, of course, they are in an "entertaining them unawares" situation and may have to ride the bus, drive a car, or call an Uber to be among people. By now, it was clear to the pastor, me, and everyone else in attendance that Jonathan had supernaturally traveled halfway around the world in the blink of an eye. And somehow, God wanted me to witness the event even if I happened to be in a different location. I mean, how cool is that?

When Jonathan did come back a few weeks later, and I had a chance to ask him about it, he said that he wasn't even aware of the episode and was sleeping at the time. God can use you and your spirit even in your sleep. Has anyone of you ever had a dream that you were somewhere unknown, maybe in a different country, in a strange culture, speaking in a language you were not familiar with? But you were there, and you ministered to someone, or you prayed healing for another? You could have traveled in the spirit that night to do something for God and were not even fully aware of it. God never sleeps even though we do.

Jesus Himself would travel in the Spirit too. When the crowd would press into Him, the bible says He would "slip away," and next thing you know, He'd be up on a mountain top alone so He could chat with the Father. God says greater works than these shall we do (John 14:12). Are you ready for some greater works? Check out some of these accounts on the matter of Spirit travel in the bible! Here we have the Apostle Paul recording a trip to Paradise:

I know a man in Christ, who fourteen years ago—whether in the body I do not know, or out of the body I do not know, God knows—such a man was caught up to the third heaven. And I know how such a man—whether in the body or apart from the body I do not know, God knows—was caught up into Paradise and heard inexpressible words, which a man is not permitted to speak (2 Corinthians 12:1-4 NASB).

And here is the account of Philip the Evangelist's divine travel experience – such a powerful testimony!

PHILIP AND THE ETHIOPIAN EUNUCH

Then an angel of the Lord said to Philip, "Get up and go toward the south to the road that goes down from Jerusalem to Gaza." (This is a wilderness road.) So, he got up and went. Now there was an Ethiopian eunuch, a court official of the Candace, queen of the Ethiopians, in charge of her entire treasury. He had come to Jerusalem to worship and was returning home; seated in his chariot, he was reading the prophet Isaiah. Then the Spirit said to Philip, "Go over to this chariot and join it." So, Philip ran up to it and heard him reading the prophet Isaiah. He asked, "Do you understand what you are reading?" He replied, "How can

I, unless someone guides me?" And he invited Philip to get in and sit beside him. Now the passage of the scripture that he was reading was this:

> "Like a sheep he was led to the slaughter,
> and like a lamb silent before its shearer, so he does not open his mouth. In his humiliation justice was denied him Who can describe his generation?
> For his life is taken away from the earth."

The eunuch asked Philip, "About whom, May I ask you, does the prophet say this, about himself or about someone else?" Then Philip began to speak, and starting with this scripture, he proclaimed to him the good news about Jesus. As they were going along the road, they came to some water; and the eunuch said, "Look, here is water! What is to prevent me from being baptized?" He commanded the chariot to stop, and both, Philip and the eunuch, went down into the water, and Philip baptized him. When they came up out of the water, the Spirit of the Lord snatched Philip away; the eunuch saw him no more, and went on his way rejoicing. But Philip found himself at Azotes, and as he was passing through the region, he proclaimed the good news to all the towns until he came to Caesarea (Acts 8:26-40 NRSV). If God can do it with Philip and Jonathan, He can do it for you and me. Is there anything too hard for the Lord?

Chapter 10

Eyes Up

I hope and pray that this book has blessed you in so many ways. I pray that it has opened your heart and eyes to see how great of a Father, Friend, and loving God we have in Him. I pray that you remember Him and His name above all things. I pray that it has created a deeper longing in you to carve out more moments in time within your own personal life to spend with Him, exploring the greatest blessing of all – our divine union with Him.

I pray that you always become aware of His constant presence around you and know that you are not divorced from His presence no matter where you are or what you are doing, whether it's praying for the sick or washing the dinner dishes or cleaning up after your kids. No matter what you are doing, I pray that you will easily and quickly respond to His promptings and invitations as you choose to share your life with Him.

When we do, we experience the benefits of being in complete union with Him. As we walk with God, we can be anchored in His love and union and remain steadfast in peace and joy even when we go through the valleys of life. When we remember that we are in Him and He is in us, we will start to notice that things just don't easily alter us negatively like they used to, that what should have taken you out didn't. When what you have been struggling with for years, even decades, healing comes suddenly out of the blue.

Sweet Holy Spirit is our very present help. Whether we realize it or not, it is true. But to have an awareness of Him is a whole other level of awesomeness. When you know that Holy Spirit is always available, that He sticks closer than a brother, that He dwells in your midst continually, that you have been pressed into by God more than you can ever spend time pressing into Him, know that we are in Christ and Christ is in us. He invaded us first! As you lean deep into this truth, you start to live life continuously out of the peace of God that passes all understanding.

That doesn't mean you won't go through things; we all will at some point that can't be avoided, but it does mean that no longer do you have to live a life of emotional turmoil and mental torture while you go through them as hard as they might be. Psalm 46:10 says, *"Be still and know that I am God."* That "be still" is for your soul where your mind and emotions reside.

In every trial and difficulty, God wants your heart, your mind, and your emotions to be still! Not up and down, left and right, forward one step and then back three. When we move into the afterlife, into eternity, who will we be leaning on and expecting to take care of all our needs? God, of course. So why not expect to go for it in the here and now? He is by far more than qualified to be the best caretaker you have ever had. If He's got you for ALL of eternity, He's got you within the boundaries of time too. We need to rest in that reality.

In all things, keep your gaze fixed on Jesus, *"the author and perfecter of our faith. For the joy set before him he endured the cross, scorning its shame, and sat down at the right hand of the throne of God"* (Hebrews 12:2).

God did not intend for you to barely get by or just be making it while you are here. No! He intended for you to thrive in every area of your life and have it to the full (John 10:10). *"Therefore, there is now no condemnation for those who are in Christ Jesus"* (Romans 8:1). There is no condemnation for you even if this picture doesn't match your current situation. So, cancel that thought but keep on believing and expecting this to become your reality as you grow in your knowledge, understanding, and relationship with God. Always...eyes up!

If you don't yet know the Lord as your own personal Lord and Savior and would like to know Him, then pray this prayer in faith and receive the free gift of salvation from God today!

Prayer: Most High God, I come to You right now as one who recognizes my need for Your grace, mercy, and forgiveness, knowing that, without You, I am lost. I ask You to forgive me of all my sins and to take Your rightful place in my heart and life as my Lord and Savior.

I believe, Jesus, that You are the Son of God. I thank You for Your ultimate sacrifice on the cross for me. I believe that You died and rose again on the third day and that You are Lord, seated in Heaven at the right hand of the Father.

I receive Your gift of salvation now, and I thank You for it in Jesus' name. Love, Your child, Amen.

If you have just prayed that prayer and believed it with your heart (Romans 10:9), then congratulations and welcome to the family of God! You have just experienced the most radical encounter of all: Salvation!

If you don't already have a bible, I would recommend getting one; you can also download a free bible app from your phone. Also, I would recommend that you get connected with a Jesus-believing community where you can learn, grow and fellowship with other members in the body of Christ.

I pray for an abundant outpouring of God's glory over your life. May you walk in the unwavering confidence of His everlasting love and goodness!

God bless you!

Thanks for reading!

If you loved the book and have a moment to share, I would really appreciate a short review as this helps new readers find my books!

Now Available!

Radical Encounters with God JOURNAL

on Amazon and other online book retail stores.

Record and keep all your encounters, dreams, visions, prophetic words and revelations all in one easy to use journal.

Or visit

www.melissarealfred.com

for more information and to also join my email list to stay connected and be the first to know about future material that will bless you

www.ingramcontent.com/pod-product-compliance
Lightning Source LLC
LaVergne TN
LVHW011714060526
838200LV00051B/2897